icons of music

Great Guitarists

icons of music

Great Guitarists

Nick Freeth
Cliff Douse

Brown
PARTWORKS

ISBN 1 84044 093 7

Produced by **Brown Partworks Ltd**
8 Chapel Place, Rivington Street, London EC2A 3DQ, UK
www.brownpartworks.co.uk

Editorial Director: Lindsey Lowe
Project Editor: Rob Dimery
Picture Researcher: Becky Cox
Production Manager: Matt Weyland

Picture Credits
Archive J.B.V.: 118; **Arena Images:** Jak Kilby 72, 100, Allan Titmuss 110, 114; **Concord Jazz:**
Bob Barry 24, Kelly Kerr 50, Mark Reiss 150; **Corbis:** Bettmann 12, 16, 54, 116, Henry Diltz
142, M. Moore 88, Denis O'Regan 108, Photoplay Archives 120, Neal Preston 36, 92, 122,
140, Roger Ressmeyer 57, Ted Williams 66; **Jill Furmanovsky:** 58; **Greg Tutmarc:** 74; **Hulton
Archives:** 60, Baron 148, Tad Hershorn 124, Frank Driggs Collection 32, 52, Metronome 84;
Hulton Getty: 70, 106, 172; **Jazz Index:** Christian Him 98, 130, Odile Noel 170, Paul Wood
42; **Dave Peabody:** 40; **Pictorial Press:** 18, 19, 28, 71, 81, 137, Escott 168, Polygram 48,
Showtime 86, Swingtime Archive 82; **Popperfoto:** 20; **Redferns:** Glenn A. Baker 94, Fin
Costello 162, Gems 8, Harry Goodwin 62, William P. Gottlieb/Library of Congress 10, 136,
Robert Knight 14, Max Jones Files 96, Michael Ochs Archives 26, 34, 38, 44, 56, 76, 112, 121,
126, 156, 166, MJF 167, Steve Morely 68, Dave Peabody 138, 154, David Redfern 64, 78, 133,
146, Ebet Roberts 144, 158, 164, Donna Santisi 104, Charlyn Zlotnik 132; **Retna:** Michael
Putland 174; **David Sinclair:** 134, 152, 160; **Sylvia Pitcher Photo Library:** 22, 46, 128, 169,
Frank Nazereth 90, The Weston Collection 80; **Paul Vidal:** 102; **Warner Brothers Records:**
Señor McGuire 30.

Front cover: Corbis/Neal Preston.
Back cover: Redferns/Charlyn Zlotnik.

Printed and bound in Hong Kong
1 2 3 4 5   06 05 04 03 02

Contents

Introduction

Mention the word "guitar" and many people will think of a Spanish guitar or perhaps a steel-strung acoustic guitar. Others may have a Fender Stratocaster in their mind's eye, while some will visualize a large archtop jazz guitar. The guitar is all of these instruments and more: it can be acoustic or electric; the strings may be plucked with the fingers or with a pick. You can even stop the strings with a slide or a bottleneck. It is used in almost every kind of music. And the people that play it are equally diverse, as this book reveals.

The guitar grew in popularity in the United States from the 1880s onward, and the modern guitar was really created in Christian Friedrich Martin's workshop in Nazareth, Pennsylvania. Much cheaper than a piano, its portability and versatility made it the instrument of choice in the parlor or on the porch. With a little application, anyone could learn a few simple chords to accompany themselves singing or to play along with a fiddle.

The Gibson Mandolin-Guitar Manufacturing Company, formed in 1902, was among the first manufacturers to fit steel strings to guitars instead of the customary gut strings. This innovation added volume, making the guitar suitable for public performance, whether indoors or on the street. The National guitar, with its inbuilt steel resonator, was introduced in 1928; it added even more volume and was popular with blues artists and itinerant musicians such as the Rev. Gary Davis during his early career. Meanwhile, the guitar had begun to replace the banjo in jazz rhythm sections and dance orchestras, and so Gibson developed the L-5, a large archtop guitar with f-holes that enabled the guitar chords to cut through the sound of the other instruments.

Eddie Lang, the pioneer of jazz guitar, helped popularize the Gibson L-5 and introduced the idea that the guitar could take solos and not merely fulfill an accompanying role. Following in Lang's footsteps, George Van Eps explored more complex harmonies on the guitar, developing a sophisticated style based largely on chords. He described the guitar as a "lap piano" and added a seventh string to give greater depth to the bass notes. The music of Eddie Lang and the influence of great jazz innovator Louis Armstrong found a resonance across the Atlantic in the virtuosic gypsy jazz of guitarist Django Reinhardt who, in turn, inspired great American players such as Les Paul, Chet Atkins, and Joe Pass.

If the early 1930s were the guitar's adolescent years, then it reached maturity in 1939 when the sound of Charlie Christian's electric guitar with the Benny Goodman Sextet and Orchestra was heard on record and on the radio. Christian's playing, with his saxlike lines, catchy riffs, and hip phrasing, inspired guitarists to escape from the servility of the rhythm section and seek the glamour of the frontline. Now they could take solos and be totally audible, with a sound that was ultracontemporary. Jazz guitarists from Barney Kessel to Wes Montgomery and from George Benson to John Scofield all owe a debt to this innovator.

The electric guitar quickly permeated all forms of American popular music and elevated the guitar ahead of all other instruments during the latter half of the twentieth century.

It inspired a succession of brilliant players in all genres, each of whom created their own particular sound and style and, in turn, influenced the next generation of guitarists.

Chicago bluesmen Elmore James and Muddy Waters used the power of the electric guitar to bring added intensity and excitement to blues performances. Buddy Guy and the King triumvirate (B.B., Albert, and Freddie) were hot on their trail. Elsewhere, Chuck Berry was combining catchy blues hooks with a solid, driving rhythm and his own savvy lyrics about teenage aspirations to create an instantly recognizable sound that fueled the rock and roll boom of the late 1950s. Many young fans were inspired to learn to play like their idols, and several, such as Eric Clapton, Peter Green, Jeff Beck, George Harrison, and Keith Richards, were to become the first generation of rock stars. From the late 1960s the energy, daring, and excitement of the playing of Jimi Hendrix pointed the way forward for later rock guitarists such as Steve Vai, Eddie Van Halen, and Brian May.

If the blues was a major factor in the development of popular music from the 1950s, so was the music of the people of rural America, with its roots in the hymns, the square dances, and the traditional songs and ballads of their European ancestors. In the 1930s, the Carter Family collected hundreds of these songs and, with their distinctive vocal harmony style and acoustic guitar accompaniment, repopularized them through radio shows. Merle Travis also pursued this path, with an advanced fingerpicking style that enabled him to pick out fiddle tunes and rags while maintaining his own accompaniment. Chet Atkins took these ideas even further and was at the epicenter of the Nashville sound from the 1950s as a guitarist, arranger, and producer for artists such as Elvis Presley and the Everly Brothers. The output of guitarists Scotty Moore, Joe Maphis, James Burton, Carl Perkins, and, over two decades later, Mark Knopfler, all reflect this fertile tradition.

From the early 1950s, a rediscovery of the earlier acoustic guitar styles revived the fortunes of bluesmen such as Big Bill Broonzy and Rev. Gary Davis. A similar folk music revival in the U.K. inspired young musicians such as Bert Jansch and John Renbourn to fuse the American acoustic guitar styles with their own traditional music and, looking farther afield, with traces of Arabic and Indian music. Simultaneously, guitarists Julian Bream and John Williams were building on the achievements of Andrés Segovia to bring classical guitar music to a wider audience.

This book tells the story of these and many other brilliant guitarists, whose creativity has helped to shape the music of today.

7

Duane Allman

1946–1971

Duane Allman and his younger brother Gregg, both avid blues fans, began playing guitar as teenagers in Daytona Beach, Florida, and became professional musicians in 1965. Two years later, they moved to Los Angeles, releasing two LPs with their band, Hour Glass; but the following year, the group split when tapes for a third album, recorded at Fame Studios in Muscle Shoals, Alabama, were rejected by their record label. The brothers returned to Florida.

However, Fame boss Rick Hall had been impressed by Duane Allman's outstanding guitar work, which drew on his early influences—guitarist B.B. King and Chuck Berry. In late 1968 Hall hired Allman as a session player, and after proving his worth at the studio, working on tracks by artists including Aretha Franklin, Wilson Pickett, and Delaney and Bonnie, Duane was invited to form a group by record company owner Phil Walden. All of its members, except percussionist Jai Johanny Johanson (a session man at Fame), were recruited from Florida: Gregg Allman on vocals and keyboards, guitarist Dickey Betts, bassist Berry Oakley, and a second drummer, Butch Trucks. Duane felt that the band needed two drummers to give it some of the punch of James Brown's group.

Named the Allman Brothers Band, the quintet began a busy gigging and recording schedule, releasing their eponymous debut album in late 1969. This captures the group's extraordinary intensity, fueled by Gregg Allman's impassioned singing and the twin lead guitars of Duane Allman and Dickey Betts—although on several tracks, notably "Dreams," it is Duane's expressive, soulful slide playing that comes to the fore. The heady mixture of blues and country that the band drew on would prove a blueprint for the sound of many bands to come, including Little Feat.

A driving, blues-based follow-up LP, *Idlewild South* (1970), was produced by Tom Dowd, who was due to start work with Eric Clapton on the album *Layla And Other Assorted Love Songs* (credited to "Derek and the Dominos") after completing the Allmans' disk. Duane asked if he could sit in on the Clapton sessions, during which he contributed his famous, wailing upper-register slide solo to "Layla" (1970). He guested on the album from which the single was picked, but rejected the offer of a permanent position in Clapton's band.

Duane resumed work with his own band, taking his dual-guitar partnership with Betts to new heights on the live double album, *The Allman Brothers Band At Fillmore East* (1971), one side of which was taken up with an epic 22-minute Gregg Allman song, "Whipping Post," featuring extended, improvised soloing. Duane started work on a new Allman Brothers Band studio album but sadly, before its completion, he was killed in a motorcycle crash near Macon, Georgia, on October 29, 1971. The group continued without him, but by a tragic coincidence, their bassist Berry Oakley died the following year after a similar accident in the same area.

Best known for his scene-stealing slide guitar work on Eric Clapton's "Layla," Duane Allman drew on the music of the Deep South to produce some of the most visceral music of the early 1970s.

Laurindo Almeida

1917–1995

Unique among guitarists, Laurindo Almeida won acclaim as a performer and as a composer in both jazz and classical music. At a time when the sound of the steel-strung acoustic and the electric guitar predominated, Almeida favored the nylon-strung Spanish guitar and introduced its softer, warm sound into jazz recordings and movie soundtracks.

He was born in São Paulo, Brazil, into a musical family (his mother was a concert pianist), and studied the guitar from childhood, playing both a classical repertoire and the popular Brazilian music of the time. The talents of the young Laurindo were quickly recognized and from the age of 14 he performed on radio broadcasts from Rio de Janeiro. In 1936 he traveled to Europe and heard the virtuoso gypsy guitarist Django Reinhardt perform in Paris—an experience that awoke Almeida's lifelong interest in jazz.

In 1947, Almeida moved to the United States and settled in Hollywood. The warm sound of his finger-picked Spanish guitar was refreshingly different to that of steel-strung acoustic and electric instruments and, with his understanding of both classical music and jazz, he was soon in demand as a studio musician, performing on movie soundtracks—his first was for *A Song Is Born* (1948)—and composer for movie scores. Almeida's guitar graced many films from the late 1940s onward, including *Viva Zapata!* (1952), *A Star Is Born* (1954), *The Old Man and the Sea* (1958), and *The Godfather* (1972). During the 1950s, he recorded 16 guitar albums that presented a wide range of repertoires, including works by South American composers such as Agustín Barrios and Heitor Villa-Lobos.

Soon after his arrival in Hollywood, an invitation to join the prestigious Stan Kenton Orchestra launched Almeida's jazz career. His solo work, showcased on the Orchestra's recordings of "Lament" and "Amazonia," caught the ear of jazz enthusiasts worldwide and established the classical guitar as a legitimate instrument in jazz. In 1953 he teamed up with saxophonist Bud Shank to record three albums entitled *Brazilliance*, blending jazz forms with Brazilian melodies and rhythms for the first time. He is widely credited with introducing the bossa nova rhythm to North America; possibly his most influential album releases were 1962's *Viva Bossa Nova*, which provided him with a Top 20 hit in the United States, and *Guitar from Ipanema* (1964). Almeida reunited with Bud Shank in 1974 to form the jazz outfit LA Four, along with bassist Ray Brown and drummer Shelly Manne (Jeff Hamilton occasionally substituted for the latter), which recorded and performed for almost two decades. Almeida and Shank also collaborated on classical projects during this period, as heard on *Selected Classical Works for Guitar and Flute* (1982).

A complete musician who bridged the classical and jazz worlds, Laurindo Almeida worked continually as a composer, arranger, and performer until his death in 1995.

Laurindo Almeida's guitar-playing prowess established him in both the jazz and classical fields, winning him a number of Grammy awards. Here he is shown performing in the 1940s.

Chet Atkins

1924–2001

Through his innovative finger-picking guitar style and his key role in the creation of hundreds of hit records, Chet Atkins became the architect of the "Nashville sound" in the 1950s and is now recognized as a major influence on the development of popular music.

Chet was raised on his father's 50-acre farm outside Luttrell, Tennessee, during the Depression. Born into a musical family—his father was a piano teacher—he was playing the ukelele by the age of five and soon graduated to the guitar. Listening to the radio, Chet became intrigued by the finger-picking style of country guitarist and singer Merle Travis, who had developed a technique of using his forefinger and thumb to play melody and rhythm at the same time. Chet began to devise his own variation on Travis's style, using combinations of two, three, and four fingers on his right hand. Later, Chet became aware of jazz, being impressed in particular by the the guitar-playing of Les Paul (with whom his brother Jim, also a guitarist, later played), George Barnes, and Charlie Christian. However, Atkins's musical skills also stretched to the fiddle, and it was as occasional fiddle player and guitarist that he secured a spot on radio station WNOX in 1942, backing comedian/vocalists Archie Campbell and Bill Carlisle.

After five years as a staff guitarist in radio, Chet was signed to the RCA label by vice-president Steve Sholes in 1947 and his first of almost 100 albums, *Chet Atkins Plays Guitar*, was released in 1951. As his style continued to develop with each new album, Chet became a revered and highly influential guitarist. Adapting a steel-guitar technique, he used artificial harmonics to create a harplike cascade of notes, an innovation that later became absorbed into the styles of jazz guitarists Lenny Breau, Martin Taylor, and Larry Coryell. From 1952, Atkins became an RCA talent scout, a task he combined with growing responsibilities as a session musician. Chet was also interested in electronics and, with recording engineers Ray Butts and Bob Ferris, introduced tone-modifying sounds that added a new dimension to the electric guitar—reverb, as heard on "Blue Ocean Echo" in 1955, tremolo in 1956, and wah-wah in 1959. By now, Chet was a mainstay of the Nashville studios, leading the sessions and playing guitar on Elvis Presley's "Heartbreak Hotel" and many Everly Brothers hits, including "Bird Dog" and "All I Have To Do Is Dream." As manager of RCA's Nashville office from 1957 and vice-president from 1968, he guided the careers of many country artists, from Don Gibson and Willie Nelson to Dolly Parton and Waylon Jennings.

Always a guitar enthusiast, Chet also found time to record duet albums with fellow guitarists Les Paul, Jerry Reed, and Mark Knopfler. He died at his home in Nashville on June 30, 2001, after a long battle with cancer.

Suaveness itself: Chet Atkins in the mid-1950s. His trademark Gretsch guitar, later known as the "Chet Atkins Country Gentleman," became an in-demand instrument in the 1960s after it was endorsed by George Harrison of The Beatles.

Jeff Beck

b.1944

Born in Surrey, England, Jeff Beck first became interested in the guitar after attending a Buddy Holly concert in early 1958, and later abandoned an art college course to become a professional musician. Graduating to studio work, he met another young session player, Jimmy Page, who, in March 1965, recommended Beck as a replacement for Eric Clapton in The Yardbirds. Whereas Clapton's approach to guitar playing had always been that of a devoted blues fan, Beck's tastes were more eclectic; one of his first contributions to the band was the haunting, sitarlike guitar part for their 1965 hit "Heart Full Of Soul."

Page joined Beck briefly in The Yardbirds during 1966—initially on bass, although he soon became the band's second guitarist. The thought of Beck and Page trading solos on stage made The Yardbirds a mouth-watering live prospect, although their dazzling guitar duels sometimes degenerated into indulgence. While the two were in the group together, they also collaborated on "Beck's Bolero," a Page composition providing Beck with an early opportunity to display his tonal range—from singing sustain to distorted, proto-heavy metal raunch. Soon after recording the track, Beck left The Yardbirds, and in March 1967 he launched The Jeff Beck Group, featuring Rod Stewart on vocals. Their powerful amalgam of rock and blues—with Beck using wah-wah to create innovative textures on songs such as "I Ain't Superstitious" (1968)—brought them substantial success, on both sides of the Atlantic. However, the band broke up in the fall of 1969, and that November, Beck was forced to put his future plans on hold after a serious car crash. At virtually the same time, Jimmy Page employed a similar formula of guitar wizardry and blues-derived sonic assaults with his new band, Led Zeppelin.

Beck was not fully fit again until 1971. Over the next two years, he launched and disbanded a new Jeff Beck Group, and subsequently formed a "power trio" with American bassist Tim Bogert and drummer Carmine Appice. Neither outfit lived up to expectations, and it was not until 1975 that Beck broke fresh musical ground with the highly acclaimed jazz-fusion album *Blow By Blow*—his biggest-selling record so far, reaching the Top 5 of the U.S. album charts. Further work in the same vein followed, including a close association with ex-Mahavishnu Orchestra keyboardist Jan Hammer, with whom Beck was to tour and record for the rest of the decade.

The 1980s and early to mid-1990s saw only a handful of solo records from Beck, who was rumored to be spending increasing amounts of time with his collection of vintage racing cars. More recently, though, he has released two CDs exploring the crossover between blues and techno—*Who Else!* (1999) and *You Had It Coming* (2001)—and looks set to continue his brilliant, unpredictable career well into the new century.

A truly maverick talent, Jeff Beck—seen here during the late 1960s—has pursued an eclectic and unpredictable career since making his name with The Yardbirds.

George Benson

b.1943

Although George Benson is best known as the successful pop artist who had hits with "Nature Boy" (1977) and "Feel Like Makin' Love" (1983), he can also play a mean guitar! In fact, he first made his living out of playing first-class jazz with some of the best players in the business. Like Herbie Hancock, Benson began his career in jazz during the 1960s and effortlessly switched over to pop during the 1970s and 1980s, before returning to his roots. In the process, he helped introduce a younger pop audience to the artful world of jazz.

George Benson was born in Pittsburgh, Pennsylvania on March 22, 1943. His stepfather was a Charlie Christian fan and he taught young George to play the ukelele and guitar. Benson made his singing debut in a local nightclub at the age of eight and by the time the youngster was 17 he was already leading his own rock and roll group. However, after hearing the seductive jazz noises of Charlie Parker and Grant Green, Benson turned his musical attention toward jazz, in particular the guitar playing of Wes Montgomery, whose licks he set about learning in his late teens. Benson developed a tone and phrasing to his style that owed much to Montgomery and was soon causing a stir on the local jazz circuit. On Green's advice, he made the move to New York, where he soon found work as a session musician. His first big break came in 1962, when the jazz organist Jack McDuff hired him to play guitar in his band. Benson left three years later to work on his own recordings including *It's Uptown* (1965), *Benson Burner* (1966), *Cookbook* (1966), and—with Herbie Hancock (piano) and Ron Carter (bass)—*Giblet Gravy* (1967). By this time Benson was well respected within jazz circles and no less a figure than the great trumpeter Miles Davis himself invited the guitarist to join his group; Benson declined, although he did play on one track on Davis's album *Miles In The Sky* (1968).

Benson was seen as the obvious choice to fill the gap left when Wes Montgomery died in 1968, but it wasn't until the mid-1970s that his record sales approached and surpassed those of his idol. Still primarily a jazz instrumentalist, Benson freely incorporated rock, pop, and soul elements during this period. *Breezin'* (1976), a U.S. chart-topper, sold more than two million units, becoming the first jazz album to go platinum. It was the first of several Grammy-winning albums Benson recorded for Warner Brothers. *In Flight* (1977) was another well-received album, featuring Benson scat singing in unison with some very fine solos. He switched to a more overtly soul-pop sound during the 1980s, with the best-selling albums *Give Me The Night* (1980), *In Your Eyes* (1983), *20/20* (1985), and *Tenderly* (1989), making him one of the most successful crossover artists of recent times. Benson's more mainstream approach was met by howls of outrage from jazz purists, but he made amends with them by recording with the Count Basie Orchestra on the LP *Big Boss Band* (1990).

George Benson is one of jazz's most technically accomplished guitarists, a fact often overlooked in the face of his considerable commercial success. He is shown here onstage in 1979.

Chuck Berry

b.1926

In 1955, Chuck Berry, a singer, guitarist, songwriter, and ex-hairdresser from St. Louis, was heard performing in a Chicago club by bluesman Muddy Waters. Impressed, Waters introduced him to record company boss Leonard Chess. Soon afterward, Berry signed to the Chess label and went into the studio with "Maybellene"—a song with a throaty opening guitar figure, lyrics about chasing a pretty girl in a fast car, and a central solo, initially dominated by a single note, that seemed to capture the sound of speed, motor horns, and revving engines. "Maybellene" was the first in a string of sharply observed, slyly executed rock and roll classics, memorable not only for their words and tunes, but also for their distinctive licks and riffs—ringing out with an almost bell-like clarity—which quickly became part of the universal currency of popular music.

Berry's hits for Chess over the following decade exuded a heady mix of fun, urgency and attitude, and featured guitar work that perfectly matched their mood. The famous (and closely related) guitar introductions to his singles "Roll Over Beethoven" (1956) and "Johnny B. Goode" (1958) have been endlessly imitated over the years, but the originals still retain their freshness, while the interplay between guitar and bass on "Memphis, Tennessee" (1959) brilliantly offsets Chuck's unusually plaintive vocals. The recordings themselves now betray their age, but lack nothing in immediacy and excitement.

It is a measure of Berry's status that his career was able to survive the adverse publicity surrounding his arrest in 1959 on the charge of "transporting a minor across a state line for immoral purposes." Berry denied the accusation, but was eventually

Above: Chuck Berry onstage during the late 1960s, resplendent in a psychedelic shirt.

convicted and imprisoned in 1962. After his release two years later, he visited the U.K. (where The Rolling Stones and The Beatles had already covered his songs), and reentered the American charts with new compositions such as "No Particular Place To Go" and "You Never Can Tell" (both 1964). However, his departure from Chess in 1966 marked the end of his long period of creative success, and although he remained popular as a live performer (enjoying a surprise transatlantic chart-topper with "My Ding-A-Ling" in 1972), he has never managed to regain the artistic momentum of his early years.

Left: A prodigiously talented songwriter and author of several classic rock and roll riffs, Chuck Berry—seen here during the mid-1950s—is one of popular music's pivotal figures.

Julian Bream

b.1933

As a child in Battersea, southwest London, Julian Bream displayed a precocious musical talent, learning jazz-style guitar from his father before taking up the classical instrument, and also playing cello and piano. He gave his first public guitar recital aged only 13, and went on to win a place at London's prestigious Royal College of Music. However, he was unable to study his chosen instrument there; at the time, few members of the musical establishment took the classical guitar seriously, and no U.K. music academy offered courses in it. Bream was obliged to focus on piano and composition instead, and on leaving the RCM in 1952, he was drafted into the British Army, spending much of the next three years playing in military-run dance bands.

After his Army service, Bream undertook various forms of guitar work, including film soundtracks and radio sessions, as well as classical concert appearances. His reputation as a performer grew rapidly throughout Europe and America, where he made his debut in 1958. He soon established himself as one of the world's leading guitar virtuosi, but unlike his more conservative colleagues, he has always shown a strong commitment to new music, commissioning or requesting guitar works from many prominent composers. Bream met Heitor Villa-Lobos in 1956, giving the composer's Guitar Concerto its British debut the following year, while Malcolm Arnold wrote a popular Guitar Concerto for Bream in 1958. Bream has also involved himself with more cutting-edge figures such as Hans Werner Henze, Sir Michael Tippett, Toru Takemitsu, and Benjamin Britten, whose "Nocturnal" (1963) has since been taken up by many other performers. This piece, based on a sixteenth-century lute-song by John Dowland, reflects another of Bream's passions: an expert lute player, as well as a guitarist, he has been influential in introducing modern audiences to the older instrument and its repertoire. Bream has premiered a number of other pieces for solo guitar and for guitar accompanied by orchestra, such as Richard Rodney Bennett's Concerto with chamber ensemble, Alan Rawsthorne's "Elegy," and Sir William Walton's "Five Bagatelles." In 1959 he founded the Julian Bream Consort, a group of musicians dedicated to reawakening interest in consort music—pre-sixteenth-century music performed by a small instrumental ensemble. He has also held a number of master classes in both the U.K. and the U.S.A.

Julian Bream's successes have won him a host of awards and honors, including an O.B.E. (Order of the British Empire) in 1968 and a C.B.E. in 1985. He has probably made and sold more records than any other classical guitarist—as evidenced by the 28-CD retrospective issued to mark his 60th birthday in 1993—and after more than half a century as a performer, he still maintains a busy schedule of tours and concert appearances.

Julian Bream's superb playing ability and appetite for new musical directions made him a true pioneer of the classical guitar in the twentieth century. He is seen here during the early 1960s.

Big Bill Broonzy

1893–1958

William Lee Conley Broonzy was born in Scott, on the banks of the Mississippi, but grew up across the river in Arkansas. As a child, he taught himself to play the fiddle (despite the disapproval of his father, a Baptist deacon), and later supplemented his income from plantation work by performing at dances and picnics. During World War I, he served with an army laboring battalion in France, returning briefly to Arkansas after the end of hostilities. However, Broonzy's experiences abroad had made him ambitious for better prospects than those offered by the Southern states, and in 1920 he moved to Chicago.

Broonzy soon found factory work in the city, and did some fiddle playing there, but by the mid-1920s he had switched to guitar, developing a crisp, ragtime-influenced technique markedly different to that of his Delta contemporaries. He made his first disks in 1926, and was in constant demand as a vocalist and instrumentalist throughout the following decade. Broonzy's work during this period was extremely diverse, encompassing novelty songs and jazzier, horn-driven material that he performed with full bands, as well as country-flavored blues. By the late 1930s, he had developed an increasingly urban and sophisticated sound, featuring piano, bass, and percussion, on records such as "Baby I Done Got Wise."

Audiences and promoters sometimes sought a more basic musical approach, and Broonzy was happy to oblige. In December 1938, billed as a "primitive blues singer," he appeared in New York at record producer John Hammond's first Carnegie Hall "Spirituals to Swing" concert, giving an acclaimed performance; in fact, he had replaced Hammond's original choice for the show, Robert Johnson, who had died a few months before. Broonzy adopted a more folk-based blues style in the years following World War II. In the early 1950s, when he was one of the first black bluesmen to gain a following among white audiences, he was playing in a countrified, less commercial style, often performing with just his guitar and a piano accompanist. Broonzy's "folk-blues" proved attractive to European jazz and traditional music fans as well as their American counterparts—he toured Europe in 1951, performing folk standards and spirituals alongside blues numbers. He was received warmly wherever he played, although many of the audiences would not have been aware of the more varied material, often performed with a band, that Broonzy had played earlier in his career. In 1955, with help from writer Yannick Bruynoghe, Broonzy published one of the first autobiographies by a blues artist, *Big Bill Blues*.

During the 1950s, Broonzy was especially popular in Britain, where he helped to pave the way for the 1960s blues boom. Sadly, he did not live to see the outcome; he was diagnosed with throat cancer in 1956, and died in Chicago on August 15, 1958.

Big Bill Broonzy played a key role in forging a link between rural blues and its electric urban cousin. He also helped guide the careers of younger blues artists, including Muddy Waters.

Kenny Burrell

b.1931

As a child in Detroit, Michigan, Kenny Burrell was surrounded by music and musicians. His father was a banjo player, his mother a pianist, and all three of his brothers were also musicians. Burrell originally wanted to play the saxophone, but the expense of the instrument encouraged him to take up the guitar instead. He studied classical guitar and received a Bachelor of Music degree from Detroit's Wayne University. He also became influenced by the pioneering jazz guitar efforts of Charlie Christian and Oscar Moore and soon developed a local reputation as a six-string virtuoso, playing with the Candy Johnson Sextet in 1948, and Dizzy Gillespie in 1951, with whom he made his first recordings. Burrell later stood in as a temporary replacement for Herb Ellis, the guitarist in Oscar Peterson's famous trio, for a six-month tour.

In 1956, Burrell moved to New York to double as a session musician and a band leader in his own right, pioneering guitar-led trios featuring drums and bass in the late 1950s. He played with Benny Goodman in 1957 and also recorded many notable jazz albums for the Blue Note, Verve, and Prestige labels, including *The Cats* (1957) with organist Jimmy Smith, *Kenny Burrell/John Coltrane* (1958) with saxophonist John Coltrane, and the superb *Guitar Forms* (1965), a critically acclaimed collaboration with composer and arranger Gil Evans. He also worked with saxophonists Stan Getz and Coleman Hawkins and pianist Tommy Flanagan (a former school friend).

In a change of direction, Burrell moved to Los Angeles during the mid-1970s to be more involved in studio work and teaching, which he continues to do to this day—he has taught History of Jazz and American Music at UCLA for more than 20 years. One of his courses, "Ellingtonia," is devoted to the life and music of jazz's most celebrated band leader, Duke Ellington. He has also recorded many jazz albums under his own name including *Live at the Village Vanguard* (1978), *Heritage* (1980), *Generations* (1987), and *Blue Lights* (1989). Despite the variety of group formats in which he has worked, Burrell ultimately prefers to explore the delicate tonal variations that can be produced from playing acoustic guitar at low volume, as he explains: "My audience has developed so that they come to listen and are quiet.… Thus I can work in a limited volume range and explore all the subtleties that can happen, which is my favorite part of the music."

Kenny Burrell has been one of the most popular jazz guitar players for more than four decades now, both as leader of his own band and as a sideman, and his smoking jazz style has been an inspiration to musicians as diverse as Pat Metheny, Van Morrison, and Elvis Costello. He was also the late Ellington's favorite guitarist—and you can't get a much better endorsement in the jazz world than that!

A versatile performer and prolific composer, Kenny Burrell has appeared on hundreds of albums, both as leader and as ensemble player. He remains one of jazz's finest ambassadors.

James Burton

b.1939

At the age of 12, James Burton received a gift from his parents that helped to determine his future career—the Fender Telecaster he had been admiring at his local music store in Shreveport, Louisiana. James put the instrument to good use: only a few years later he was playing regularly for the *Louisiana Hayride*, a radio show broadcast every Saturday night from Shreveport and heard all over the South. Despite his youth, Burton was already talented enough to back major country stars such as Slim Whitman and George Jones on the show.

In 1957, Burton's guttural, blues-inspired guitar on Dale Hawkins's rock and roll classic "Suzie Q" brought him his first hit record. A year later, following a move to Los Angeles, Burton began a six-year stint with singer Ricky Nelson, then a teen idol, providing distinctive solo work on major hits such as "Believe What You Say" (1958) and "Hello Mary Lou" (1961). On his recordings with Nelson, Burton would often make use of his trademark "chicken pickin'"—a damped, staccato right-hand style that has been widely emulated by other performers. Burton's style owed much to Carl Perkins and Scotty Moore, both of whom demonstrated a crossover between country and rock and roll in their guitar playing.

By the time Burton left Nelson in 1964, he had established himself as one of America's most respected guitarists. After several years of successful session playing, during which he worked with artists as diverse as Buffalo Springfield, Ry Cooder, Randy Newman, Judy Collins, Joni Mitchell, and John Phillips of the Mamas and the Papas, he accepted his highest-profile job to date, as guitarist for Elvis Presley. Burton stayed with the King from 1969 until 1977, but he and other Elvis sidemen also found time to collaborate with singer-songwriter Gram Parsons on his albums *GP* (1973), and *Grievous Angel* (1974). These records featured the still unknown Emmylou Harris on vocals, and following Parsons's death in 1973, Burton and his Presley colleagues (including the pianist Glen D. Hardin, once one of Buddy Holly's Crickets) formed the core of Emmylou's Hot Band, contributing to her classic early LPs such as *Pieces Of The Sky* (1975) and *Elite Hotel* (1976). Burton's style drew heavily on the rockabilly that he had been playing since his youth, and was itself influential on the harder country sound that Merle Haggard created during the late 1960s and early 1970s. However, though undoubtedly powerful, his solos were always tasteful, never overtly demonstrative.

Burton subsequently left the Hot Band to return to session playing, which has remained his major activity ever since—although he has also toured extensively with star names such as the late John Denver and Jerry Lee Lewis. Now recovered from an accident in 1995 that threatened to deprive him of the use of his hands, he has recently appeared throughout the world in "Elvis—The Concert," a show in which he and other Presley band members provide live backing for a video-projection of their former leader.

Drawing on his rockabilly roots, Burton developed a distinctive, staccato guitar-picking style. His extensive session work was highly influential in the development of country rock.

Charlie Byrd

Charlie Byrd recorded more than 100 guitar albums during a successful career that spanned more than half a century. Along with legendary tenor saxophonist Stan Getz, he helped establish the bossa nova and samba rhythms on a global scale. He was also the first guitarist to fuse Latin, classical, and jazz styles into a commercially successful package.

Byrd was born in Chuckatuck, Virginia, on September 16, 1925. His father and three brothers were all guitarists and Charlie followed in the family tradition, starting to learn guitar and mandolin at the age of 10, and becoming a proficient guitarist by the time he had reached his early teens. During World War II, he toured Europe with an army show band and it was there that he met renowned gypsy guitarist Django Reinhardt. After the war, Byrd moved to Washington D.C., where he temporarily switched his musical attentions over to classical music, studying with Sophocles Papas, a respected classical guitar teacher. Byrd also attended an Andrés Segovia master class in Siena, Italy, during the summer of 1954, to expand his knowledge of classical guitar.

During the 1950s, Byrd toured with Woody Herman's band and also formed his own group, which allowed him to draw on both his jazz and classical influences. Toward the end of the decade, Byrd accepted an invitation from the U.S. State Department to tour South America. During his visit, he became aware of the burgeoning bossa nova movement, a musical style created by songwriter Antonio Carlos Jobim and singer João Gilberto that drew on both Brazilian samba rhythms and the "cool jazz" of the West Coast. Byrd's discovery was to mark a major turning point in his career. Inspired partly by guitarist Laurindo Almeida's early work with Brazilian rhythms, Byrd subsequently formed a much-celebrated collaboration with Stan Getz on *Jazz Samba* (1962). The recording, featuring some exceptional compositions by Brazilian composers such as Antonio Carlos Jobim and João Gilberto, was an instant best-seller, sparking off a bossa nova craze across the Western world. Byrd's success continued with a string of solo albums including *Solo Flight* (1965), *Brazilian Byrd* (1965), and *Charlie Byrd Plays Villa-Lobos* (1967).

Byrd's career attracted widespread attention again in 1973, when he teamed up with two other jazz guitarists, Barney Kessel and Herb Ellis, to form Great Guitars. They performed regularly together throughout the 1970s and 1980s in both America and Europe. Meanwhile, Byrd continued to record as a solo artist, producing a variety of guitar albums including *Brazilville* (1981), *Isn't It Romantic* (1984), and *The Bossa Nova Years* (1991). He gave his last performance in Annapolis, Maryland, on September 18, 1999, and died from cancer just three months later.

Charlie Byrd was one of the few jazz guitarists to use an unamplified nylon-strung jazz acoustic guitar as well as an amplified instrument. Along with saxophonist Stan Getz, Byrd was primarily responsible for introducing the bossa nova sound to a wider audience.

Larry Carlton

b.1948

Larry Carlton took studio guitar playing to new heights during the late 1970s and early 1980s. While most other session musicians of the day were churning out predictable guitar licks for their rock and jazz employers, Carlton was supplying his clients with lead lines that can only be described as sublime. His solo style, a sophisticated mixture of jazz, blues, and rock, was an important feature on many major albums from this period.

Larry was born in Torrance, California on March 2, 1948. As a child, he showed precocious musical talent, began taking music lessons at the age of six, and was playing the guitar competently at 10. Later, as a teenager, he became influenced by blues players B.B. King, Robben Ford, and Albert Collins, and jazz guitarists Wes Montgomery, Joe Pass, and Barney Kessel. He started working professionally as a session musician in the late 1960s and played with renowned jazz pianist George Shearing during this period. He joined The Crusaders (formerly The Jazz Crusaders) in 1971, and they released a string of popular albums including *The Second Crusade* (1972), *Unsung Heroes* (1973), *Chain Reaction* (1975), and the critically acclaimed *Free As The Wind* (1977). It was with The Crusaders that Carlton developed the rhythmic, bluesy style with which he is most readily associated.

Larry left the Crusaders in 1976 to pursue a career as a solo guitarist and session musician. His experience of a wide variety of musical genres stood him in good stead, enabling him to adapt to pop, rock, or jazz with equal ease. His innovative guitar playing is heard throughout Steely Dan's 1976 album *The Royal Scam*; the standout, fluid solo on "Kid Charlemagne" was later rated by *Rolling Stone* magazine as one of the three best licks in rock. His popular album *Larry Carlton* (1978) featured a catchy instrumental, "Room 335," on which Carlton played a superb solo on a Gibson ES335 guitar, which produced a characteristic sweet, creamy sound. Subsequently, fans and guitar magazines began to dub him "Mr. 335," while Carlton himself dubbed his home recording studio "Room 335." He later recorded a string of classic guitar albums, including *Mr. 335 Live In Japan* (1979), *Strikes Twice* (1980), *Discovery* (1987), *Kid Gloves* (1992), and *No Substitutions: Live In Osaka* (2001).

Despite his stature as a solo artist, Carlton is probably most respected for his exceptional studio guitar work; in his heyday as a session musician in the 1970s he was playing on up to 500 albums per year. As a sideman, he has played with Joni Mitchell, Michael Jackson, Quincy Jones, Sammy Davis Jr., Diana Ross, Linda Ronstadt, and Art Garfunkel among others. His sparse, tasteful licks on Steely Dan's *Gaucho* (1980) and Donald Fagan's *The Nightfly* (1982) are considered by audiophiles to be among the finest recorded moments in musical history.

A true musician's musician. The distinctive sweet sound of Larry Carlton's Gibson ES335 has graced literally thousands of albums, during more than 30 years of session work.

Maybelle Carter

1909–1978

Maybelle Addington was born in Nickelsville, southwest Virginia. As a child, she sang and played guitar, banjo, and autoharp with a number of friends and relatives, including her cousin Sara Dougherty, who, in 1915, married Alvin Pleasant Carter, a fruit tree salesman and part-time singer from nearby Maces Spring. Eleven years later, the couple formed a trio with Maybelle, following her marriage to A.P.'s brother, Ezra (who was not a musician); in 1927, the new group, featuring all three Carters on vocals, Maybelle on guitar, and Sara on autoharp and occasional second guitar, traveled to Tennessee to see if they could find themselves a record contract.

The Carter Family made their first recordings at an audition for Victor Records in Bristol, Tennessee, on August 1, 1927 and were offered a recording contract shortly afterward. These early sessions produced several items that subsequently became country music classics, such as "Wildwood Flower" and "Keep On The Sunny Side"; the trio went on to record more than 300 songs, including traditional material, sentimental ballads, and gospel numbers. The Carter Family's style of performance varied little throughout their career, and Maybelle's guitar work was a mainstay of their sound. She played a Gibson L-5 archtop, often tuning it a half step lower than normal, and using the thumb on her right hand to pick out melodies on the bass strings while her fingers strummed chords in the treble. This so-called "thumb-brush" technique added variety and rhythmic impetus to the group's distinctive harmony singing, and was so widely copied that it was later renamed "Carter picking." Although it is as a guitarist that she is remembered today, Maybelle was a fine singer in her own right, harmonizing with her cousin's lead vocal. A.P., the possessor of a soft baritone voice, occasionally added a third harmony.

The trio's reputation spread rapidly as a result of their recordings and radio broadcasts, and they continued to work together until 1943, when Sara decided to retire. Maybelle subsequently formed a new group with her three daughters, Anita, Helen, and June. They appeared regularly at Nashville's Grand Ole Opry throughout the 1950s, accompanied by the young Chet Atkins, before joining the Johnny Cash roadshow in 1961. The same year saw Maybelle record an album of old Carter Family songs with guitarist Lester Flatt and banjo player Earl Scruggs. Cash, who married June Carter seven years later, described his new mother-in-law as "one of the most influential instrumentalists in country music."

In 1972, Maybelle was among the many distinguished performers who guested on the Nitty Gritty Dirt Band's triple LP *Will The Circle Be Unbroken*—the title track, on which she sang lead, is an old Carter Family song. Maybelle continued to perform until her death, in Nashville, on October 23, 1978.

Country music's first family. From left to right: Maybelle, A.P., and Sara. The trio pioneered country harmony singing, their distinctive sound enhanced by Maybelle's innovative guitar playing.

Charlie Christian

1916–1942

Charlie Christian was a pioneer who helped bring the electric guitar to the forefront of jazz and, indeed, popular music. His style of playing, particularly his single-note runs, influenced all of the major jazz guitarists of the 1940s, 1950s, and 1960s—so, just about every bit of jazz guitar you're likely to hear will have been influenced by him in one way or another.

Charles Henry Christian was born in Bonham, Texas, on July 29, 1916. He grew up in Oklahoma City with his musical parents—his father was a singer and his mother a pianist—and, after an initial spell on the trumpet, started playing the guitar when he was 12, building his first instrument out of cigar boxes. The family often worked as street musicians, with Christian senior singing to the accompaniment of Charlie and his brothers Clarence (mandolin) and Edward (string bass). Charlie later played guitar in his brothers' band, The Jolly Jugglers, but it wasn't until he joined the Anna Mae Winburn Orchestra in 1937 that his talents gained wider recognition. Around that time he met another guitarist, Eddie Durham, who played an early amplified guitar (as heard on a 1935 recording, Jimmie Lunceford's "Hittin' The Bottle"); Charlie decided to try an amplified instrument for himself, a Gibson ES-150, the best guitar that the market could offer at the time. He mastered it within a year and became the first established electric guitar virtuoso in jazz, playing saxophone-like lead lines and augmented and diminished chords in a way that was later to become a part of the standard jazz repertoire, and transforming the guitar into a lead instrument in its own right. His lead guitar playing was inspired in particular by the lengthy solos of Lester Young, the tenor saxophonist; the two were to play together in John Hammond's 1939 "Spirituals to Swing" concert.

Charlie hit the big time when he successfully auditioned for Benny Goodman's band late in 1939; apparently, an initially skeptical Goodman was so astonished by the young guitarist's ability that he allowed the first number they played together to run for more than half an hour. Charlie spent two years with Goodman, and his electric guitar gave the band a vibrant new sound that coincided with the beginning of the 1940s. He would also play late nights at Minton's Playhouse in Harlem, delivering astounding improvisations. Players such as trumpeter Dizzie Gillespie and pianist Thelonious Monk were often in the audience. It was at Minton's that Charlie took some of the first steps toward bebop, as heard on the live recording "Swing To Bop," featuring Gillespie and drummer Kenny Clarke.

Unfortunately, Charlie struggled to adjust to the sudden success that had come his way. He drank a lot of alcohol during those late nights and hardly slept, despite warnings from his doctor. By 1941 he became ill with tuberculosis during a tour of the U.S. Midwest. He died in the Seaview Sanitorium, Staten Island, on March 2, 1942.

Despite the brevity of his performing career, Charlie Christian's stunning improvisatory skills played a major part in transforming the electric guitar into a lead instrument.

Eric Clapton

b.1945

Eric Clapton's rise through the ranks of the London music scene began when he left art college to join R&B band The Roosters in 1963. His next group was The Yardbirds, with whom he played R&B and blues. (Yardbirds manager Giorgio Gomelsky nicknamed Clapton "Slowhand," partly as an ironic reference to the guitarist's blistering speed.) But Clapton opposed the increasingly commercial nature of the band's output, typified by their 1964 hit single "For Your Love," and quit in 1965 to become lead guitarist for John Mayall's Bluesbreakers. In 1966, Clapton caused a minor revolution by declining to turn his amplifier down during sessions for *John Mayall's Bluesbreakers With Eric Clapton,* thus becoming one of the first British players to capture his guitar tone on record in all its raw, distorted glory.

Clapton's work with Mayall marked a distinct improvement on his playing from his Yardbirds days. He could extract a mellow, warm tone from his Gibson Les Paul at low volume, but with the amplifier cranked up, Clapton might produce a dynamic, biting attack or a soaring, sustained wail. His brilliance and versatility as a performer prompted the graffito "Clapton is God," which began to appear on London subway walls in the 1960s.

In mid-1966, Clapton formed Cream with bassist Jack Bruce and drummer Ginger Baker. The earliest rock "supergroup," they played with unprecedented virtuosity, and gave themselves space for extended soloing, which Clapton filled impressively on tracks such as Robert Johnson's "Crossroads" from *Wheels Of Fire* (1968). However, the trio survived for barely two years, and after an unsatisfying stint with Baker, Stevie Winwood (ex-Traffic), and Rich Grech (ex-Family) in another supergroup, Blind Faith, Clapton launched his solo career in 1970. He made two LPs (including the classic *Layla And Other Assorted Love Songs*, with guest guitarist Duane Allman) before spending an extended period out of the limelight, during which he battled to conquer an addiction to heroin.

His drug-free reemergence coincided with a change in his guitar sound—he now favored a lighter-toned Fender Stratocaster in preference to the Les Pauls that had been his choice in Cream—and a growing musical eclecticism. Subsequently, the ex-blues purist was to perform and record reggae—most famously on "I Shot The Sheriff" (1974)—romantic ballads, and film soundtracks. This diversification has sometimes been criticized, especially by Clapton's older fans. But overall, it has paid rich artistic dividends, and given audiences the chance to hear him in revealing new contexts. *Unplugged* (1992), for example, showcased his often-overlooked acoustic guitar playing. The success of Clapton's straight blues projects, such as *From The Cradle* (1994), and his collaborations with B.B. King and other masters of the genre, are proof of his unwavering commitment to the music that made him famous.

Eric Clapton became the U.K.'s first blues guitar hero in the 1960s. "He'd conjure up these incredible moods and intensity," recalls John Mayall. "The things he did with a slow blues—when he felt like playing a slow blues—could send shivers down your spine."

Eddie Cochran

1938–1960

As a child in Oklahoma City, Eddie Cochran toyed with the idea of becoming a drummer or a trombonist before taking up the guitar at the age of 12, teaching himself how to play the instrument by listening to country and western songs on the radio. A few years later, the Cochran family moved to Bell Gardens, in the Los Angeles area, where, by 1955, Eddie was already performing as one half of the country-flavored "Cochran Brothers" duo; his (unrelated) partner, Hank Cochran, would later make a name for himself in Nashville. After splitting from Hank in 1956, Eddie began collaborating with songwriter Jerry Capehart, who subsequently became his manager. Their early efforts included Cochran's unsuccessful debut single, "Skinny Jim" (1956), as well as occasional film music sessions. One such session led to Cochran's appearance in the Jayne Mansfield movie *The Girl Can't Help It* (1956), during which he sang "Twenty Flight Rock." Shortly afterward, he was signed by Liberty Records, and, after a bit part in another film, *Untamed Youth* (1956), his solo career began to take off in earnest.

Eddie's first single for Liberty, "Sittin' in the Balcony" (1957), was, unusually, not his own composition; it was written by John D. Loudermilk, later responsible for 1960s classics such as "Break My Mind." It reached number 18 in the U.S. charts, and was followed into the hit parade in 1958 by "Summertime Blues"—a classic Cochran/Capehart number about teenage summer frustration, driven by a memorable acoustic guitar part enhanced with overdubbing and handclaps. Eddie's next single, "C'mon Everybody" (1958), was similarly tailor-made for American youth—this time the subject was holding a house party while your parents are away. Like its predecessor, the track featured some powerful, up-front acoustic playing, but Cochran was equally skillful on electric guitar, as his bold soloing and subtle accompaniment on tracks such as "Jeannie, Jeannie, Jeannie" (1958) demonstrate.

At his happiest when composing and recording—he was in his element in the studio and had already proved himself adept at overdubbing instruments—Cochran was less enthusiastic about his grueling tour commitments, particularly after the death of his friend Buddy Holly in February 1959. However, he enjoyed traveling with his girlfriend Sharon Sheeley, cowriter of one of his last great songs, "Somethin' Else" (1959), and, in early 1960, he asked her to join him in the U.K., where he had been performing with Gene Vincent. Cochran and Vincent were the first U.S. rockers to tour the U.K. and were received rapturously wherever they played. On April 17, the three Americans were sharing a taxi to London Airport after a concert in Bristol when it was involved in an accident. Sheeley and Vincent were seriously hurt, but survived; Cochran died from his injuries.

Eddie Cochran created some of the best-sounding classics of rock and roll, vignettes of teenage angst driven by urgently strummed acoustic guitars and bright, lively electric lead.

Ry Cooder

b.1947

Ry Cooder excels on a number of fretted instruments, from the mandolin to the tiple (a small guitar), but is best known for his mastery of the slide guitar. Initially acclaimed for his blues-influenced playing, he has also embraced many other musical styles, and has been involved in a range of rewarding collaborations with folk and "roots" performers from the U.S. and beyond.

Cooder began playing the guitar at the age of three, mastering the instrument largely through his own efforts. The blues made a huge impact on the young guitarist; he was particularly influenced by Josh White, a New York-based folk-blues singer and guitarist. Cooder spent many of his teenage years playing at the Ash Grove, the hub of the blues scene in Los Angeles, his home city; his professional debut came in 1964, backing singer Jackie DeShannon. After brief stints with the Rising Sons (featuring Taj Mahal) and Captain Beefheart's Magic Band (he played on Beefheart's classic 1967 debut album *Safe As Milk*), Cooder became a successful Hollywood-based session musician, and during 1968/9 he visited London, guesting on several Rolling Stones recording dates (the results appeared on 1969's *Let It Bleed* and 1971's *Sticky Fingers*).

In 1970, Cooder launched his solo career with the first of several LPs exploring sometimes obscure aspects of blues, jazz, and other genres. These early records featured contributions from a wide variety of performers (bluesman Sleepy John Estes, conjunto accordionist Flaco Jimenez, and a core of top L.A. session men), with Cooder providing his trademark guitar and vocals. Later solo albums retained a distinctive musical approach, but moved closer to the mainstream and included self-compositions; however, in the 1980s albums became less frequent, as Ry became increasingly attracted to film soundtrack work.

His first movie score, making impressive use of traditional songs and tunes, was for *The Long Riders* (1980), directed by Walter Hill, which told the story of the James Gang. Hill and Cooder have collaborated on several subsequent film projects, such as *Southern Comfort* (1981) and *Last Man Standing* (1996); among Cooder's other notable soundtracks is his darkly atmospheric music for Wim Wenders's *Paris, Texas* (1984).

By the 1990s, after many years of championing American folk styles, Cooder sought musical stimulus further afield, making Grammy-award-winning albums with Indian instrumental virtuoso V.M. Bhatt (*A Meeting By The River*, 1993), who plays the mohan vina (an Indian version of the steel guitar), and Malian guitarist Ali Farka Toure (*Talking Timbuktu*, 1994). In 1996 he produced and played on the hugely successful *Buena Vista Social Club*, recorded in Havana with veteran Cuban musicians including singer Ibrahim Ferrer and pianist Ruben González.

Ry Cooder's long career has seen him embrace a range of musical styles, including psychedelia, American folk music, blues, and, more recently, world music.

Robert Cray

b.1953

Robert Cray's singing and playing draws on a wide range of rock and soul influences, but is unmistakably part of the blues tradition. His first serious exposure to the music came in 1969, when, as a schoolboy in Virginia, he heard guitarist Albert Collins (known as "the Iceman," and famous for his use of minor keys and stinging riffs) at a pop festival. Cray, already an accomplished player, began to study the older man's style and learn some of his material. Their paths crossed again when Collins performed at Cray's high school graduation dance in 1971, and during the mid-1970s, an early incarnation of the Robert Cray Band served a stint as Collins's backing group. Cray's smooth, clean playing style also owes much to original Fleetwood Mac guitarist Peter Green, another of his formative influences.

Cray's reputation grew steadily on the U.S. blues scene, but he suffered a setback when Tomato, the company that released his debut album, *Who's Been Talkin'* (1980), went out of business shortly after its appearance. Nevertheless, the LP, showcasing Cray's crisp, nimble Stratocaster licks, brought plaudits from senior blues figures such as Muddy Waters and John Lee Hooker, both of whom shared concerts with him in the early 1980s. Cray had matured both as a musician and as a songwriter by the time of his next release, *Bad Influence* (1983), and whereas his debut album had contained several cover versions, this new release was primarily Cray-penned.

In 1985, Robert was reunited with Albert Collins and fellow bluesman Johnny Copeland for the Grammy-winning *Showdown!* However, his real commercial breakthrough came with *Strong Persuader* (1986). The album's soulful feel and Cray's taut, fiery guitar work gave him his first million seller, and the LP went on to become the most successful blues release for more than 20 years. The introduction of a brass section—The Memphis Horns—further distinguished the album from previous Cray releases, bringing the sound closer to that of a Stax record.

Strong Persuader established Cray as the most commercially successful blues artist to emerge for decades. Over the following years he has maintained this preeminence, keeping the respect of the genre's surviving elder statesmen, many of whom have recorded with him or appeared alongside him. While the blues remain the cornerstone of his work, Cray has relished his occasional excursions into pop and rock with artists such as Keith Richards, Tina Turner, and Eric Clapton—Clapton has long respected Cray's work, covering his song "Bad Influence" and inviting him onstage during his series of concerts at the Royal Albert Hall in 1989. Perhaps Cray's only detractors are the purists who criticize his catholicity of taste, arguing that such diversity weakens the force of the blues in his music. However, after more than 25 years as a bandleader, and a string of hit records that shows every sign of continuing, Cray can be confident that his musical approach is the right one.

Robert Cray's clean, fluid guitar playing and warm vocals have made for a winning formula. His commercial success has helped reawaken interest in the blues and the work of elder blues legends.

Steve Cropper

b.1941

Steve Cropper was born in Willow Spring, Missouri, but only became seriously interested in music after his family moved to Memphis when he was nine. He took up guitar five years later, and was soon absorbing a wide range of stylistic influences from radio and records—his favorites included Chuck Berry, Chet Atkins, and jazzman Tal Farlow. While still in high school, Cropper cofounded his first band, the Royal Spades.

In 1961, Cropper and several other Royal Spades were among a group of performers who recorded the single "Last Night" under the name of the Mar-Keys. Released on Memphis's Satellite (later Stax) label, it became a surprise Top 3 hit. The band went on to play regular gigs as the Mar-Keys, but Steve, now a college student, eventually left to become a musician and occasional engineer at Stax. There, in the summer of 1962, Cropper, organist Booker T. Jones, and a group of session men later known as the MGs (standing for "Memphis Group") used some studio downtime to cut an impromptu instrumental, "Green Onions." Originally conceived as a B-side (to the single "Behave Yourself"), it went on to reach number 3 in the U.S. singles chart, and is now one of the most famous pop instrumentals of all time. Jones's punchy keyboards were doubtless one of the elements in the record's success, but Cropper's clipped snatches of treble-heavy lead guitar also made a memorable contribution.

As the label's resident backing band, the MGs (who enjoyed several further hits in their own right during the 1960s and early 1970s) effectively created the "Stax sound," familiar from a string of subsequent soul classics. Steve Cropper's crisp, staccato Telecaster chords and terse, tightly coiled lead figures were among its key ingredients. Cropper also took a significant role in many other aspects of the studio's success, becoming a skilled producer as well as a guitarist. He also arranged or cowrote several of the celebrated songs on which he played, including Wilson Pickett's "In The Midnight Hour" (1965), Eddie Floyd's "Knock On Wood" (1966), and Otis Redding's "(Sittin' On) The Dock Of The Bay" (1968).

Since leaving Stax in 1970, Cropper has remained active as a performer and producer. After his Memphis-based studio TMI folded in the early 1970s, he relocated to L.A., where he busied himself with production and session-playing duties, featuring prominently on Rod Stewart's hit album *Atlantic Crossing* (1975). Today Cropper is the owner of a major Nashville studio. He is also famous for his membership of the Blues Brothers Band (along with MGs' bassist Donald "Duck" Dunn). The guitarist appeared in both the original 1970s Blues Brothers line-up that included John Belushi, and with the group's more recent incarnation, featuring John Goodman.

Steve Cropper's lean, economical lead guitar playing was a key feature of the MGs' sound and, by implication, the sound of Stax Records.

Rev. Gary Davis

1896–1972

Born in Laurens, South Carolina, Gary Davis was raised on a farm by his grandmother. He was playing harmonica, banjo, and guitar by the age of about seven, and as a teenager, he performed at dances and picnics with local string bands. Davis had begun to lose his sight in infancy, and as the condition worsened he spent a brief spell at an institute for the blind in nearby Spartanburg, following which he began working as an itinerant street musician, developing a distinctive repertoire of blues and dance numbers during his subsequent travels throughout the Southeast. By age 30 he was completely blind.

In 1933, Davis, now based in Durham, North Carolina, became a minister of the Free Baptist Connection Church; but although his new-found faith was strongly reflected in the gospel that became a feature of most of his songs, he never entirely abandoned the blues, or the other secular elements of his musical style, including rags and turn-of-the-century square dances. His singing and playing were always fervent and powerful, and his guitar work, with its expressive bending, fast, crisp runs, and occasional crowd-pleasing touches—such as the bugle-calls, muted glissandos and gunshot effects in his virtuoso "Civil War March"—must have created a sensation on the sidewalks where he performed.

During his period in Durham, Davis teamed up with another talented finger-picking blues player, called Blind Boy Fuller. In 1935, the two traveled to New York together to record for the American Record Company, for whom Robert Johnson was to record the following year. Davis featured a selection of blues and gospel material (including "Twelve Gates To The City" and "I Am The True Vine") on his first recording sessions; sadly, a dispute with his producer kept him out of the studio for the next decade.

Davis finally left Durham in the 1940s, moving to New York, where he joined a Baptist church in Harlem, and sang and played on the streets of the city. He made LPs for several companies during this period, but remained relatively obscure until the early 1960s, when the "folk revival" brought him an enthusiastic new audience. His appearances at New York coffeehouses and folk clubs such as Gerde's Folk City brought him to the attention of folk-blues artists such as Dave Van Ronk and the young Bob Dylan.

For the rest of his life, Rev. Davis and "Miss Gibson," his trademark Gibson J-200 guitar, were in regular demand at concerts and festivals all over the U.S. and U.K. His first visit to British shores came in 1964 with the Blues and Gospel Caravan; the same year, he was a subject of a short film, entitled simply *Blind Gary Davis*. He also attracted the attention of many younger musicians (notably guitarist and teacher Stefan Grossman) who were eager to learn from him, and have continued to spread the word about his "holy blues" in the years since his death, from a heart attack, at the age of 76.

A powerful singer and accomplished performer on both the six-string and 12-string guitar, Rev. Gary Davis seamlessly combined sacred and secular influences in his music.

Duane Eddy

Born in Corning, New York, Duane Eddy developed an early passion for the guitar and for country music. By his mid-teens, when he and his family were living in Coolidge, Arizona, he had become a regular visitor to local radio station KCKY, and had struck up a friendship with a young DJ, Lee Hazlewood. Soon, Eddy was singing and playing on KCKY, and his working relationship with Hazlewood continued after both men moved northwest to Phoenix, where Lee was keen to start a career as a record producer.

Hazlewood and Eddy had already collaborated on an unsuccessful vocal single, "Soda Fountain Girl" (1956), but now decided to change tack and search for a new, distinctive instrumental sound. They found it while experimenting at a tiny Phoenix studio, Ramsey's Recorders, where Lee had the idea of taking the amplified signal from Duane's guitar and feeding it through an old watertank he had salvaged from a nearby junkyard. The effect worked best when Duane confined himself to the bass strings of his Gretsch 6120 semiacoustic, and the resultant "twang" (soon to become his musical trademark) made its first appearance on "Movin' 'N' Groovin'" (1958). It was a minor hit, but the follow-up, "Rebel Rouser" (1958), characterized by heavy echo and tremolo on Eddy's guitar, reached number 6 in the charts and went on to become his first million-selling release. The track established the reputations of both Duane and Lee (guitarist and producer usually shared composing credits on Duane's records), and attracted the attention of another young producer, Phil Spector, who visited the Phoenix studio to see for himself how that distinctive guitar sound was being created.

Guitar instrumentals were very much in vogue during the late 1950s and early 1960s—Bill Justis's "Raunchy" and Link Wray's "Rumble" were major hits in 1958, while Cliff Richard's backing group, The Shadows, were soon to become the most popular group in the U.K. with a string of guitar-led smashes. However, with his swinging, bassy riffs, Duane Eddy rapidly established himself as guitar king. Eddy's numerous subsequent hits (his biggest seller was the theme to the movie *Because They're Young*, released in 1960, which gave him a Top 5 hit on both sides of the Atlantic) owed their effectiveness not just to his instantly recognizable playing and Hazlewood's production, but to his excellent backing musicians, The Rebels, who also accompanied him on tour.

Eddy remained a popular live attraction in the U.S. and (especially) the U.K. even after his chart successes dried up in the mid-1960s, and enjoyed a spectacular comeback in 1986 when he joined the innovative British group The Art of Noise in a remake of his 1959 instrumental "Peter Gunn," which made the U.K. Top 10. In 1994, Duane Eddy was inducted into the Rock and Roll Hall of Fame.

The king of twang. Duane Eddy's distinctive guitar sound, backed by his tight, fiery backing band The Rebels, graced a string of classic rock and roll instrumental hits.

Herb Ellis

b.1921

Herb Ellis was born in Farmersville, Texas on August 4, 1921. He began teaching himself to play the harmonica and banjo as a child and took up the guitar at the age of 10, inspired by Charlie Christian's recordings with the Benny Goodman Orchestra. He studied at North Texas State College, majoring in bass violin because there were no guitar tutors there at the time. After graduation, Ellis played in a number of bands including the Casa Loma Orchestra and the Jimmy Dorsey Big Band, while the next few years saw him appear on several recordings by Louis Armstrong. In 1947, he formed his own trio, Soft Winds, with a Nat King Cole format featuring pianist Lou Carter and bassist/violinist Johnny Frigo. All three players sang in harmony and in many ways their sound anticipated that of the later well-known vocal group, The Four Freshmen.

Ellis came to prominence as a guitar player in 1953 when he took Barney Kessel's place in the celebrated Oscar Peterson Trio. His bluesy guitar style, incorporating something of a country twang, was directly influenced by Charlie Christian and contrasted sharply with Kessel's more bebop-oriented approach. The trio was together for five years, until Herb left to work with Ella Fitzgerald and, later, Julie London. Some jazz fans maintain that pianist Oscar Peterson, bassist Ray Brown, and Ellis were the finest piano trio of all time. Ellis's encounter with Ray Brown led to a professional working relationship and personal friendship that has endured ever since.

Ellis recorded a number of his own blues-influenced albums during this period, including *Ellis In Wonderland* (1956), *Nothing But The Blues* (1957), his personal favorite, *Herb Ellis Meets Jimmy Giuffre* (1959), and *Thank You, Charlie Christian* (1960). During the 1960s, Ellis was in great demand as a guitarist for TV and jingle music. However, he also established himself on the West Coast as a session musician, working with Charlie Byrd, among other artists.

Ellis often collaborated with other guitar players and, during the early 1970s, he formed duos with Joe Pass, Freddie Green, and Barney Kessel, before deciding to form a trio with Kessel and the Latin-influenced Charlie Byrd. The three called themselves the Great Guitars and it was easy to see why: Ellis's blues-influenced approach complemented both Kessel's straight-ahead jazz style and Byrd's relaxed easy-listening feel; between the three of them, they covered a very wide range of musical styles.

The 1980s and 1990s saw the release of a number of Herb Ellis albums, mostly on the Concord and Justice labels, including *Herb Mix* (1981), *Doggin' Around* (1988), *Roll Call* (1991), and *Down Home* (1991).

Herb Ellis first came to prominence as a member of Oscar Peterson's trio in the early 1950s. Since that time, his individually bluesy take on jazz, inspired originally by Charlie Christian, has established him as one of the genre's finest practitioners.

Tal Farlow

1921–1998

Tal Farlow was, without a doubt, one of the greatest jazz guitarists of all time. His stunning solos explored new territory and his unstoppable swing breathed life into any tune he played. He was also the first guitarist to be able to play a harmonic note on every fret of the instrument. Few guitarists to this day have mastered this technique.

Talmadge Holt Farlow was born in Greensboro, North Carolina on June 7, 1921. He was born into a musical family—his father played the ukelele, banjo, guitar, and violin—and started to learn the guitar at the age of eight. His earliest influences came from hillbilly players, but as soon as he heard the revolutionary electric guitar sound of Charlie Christian during the late 1930s, he switched over to jazz. Farlow initially worked as a sign painter and only saw his guitar playing as a hobby, but it reached a sufficiently high standard for vibraphonist Marjorie Hyams to hire him in 1948. A year later he formed the now legendary musical relationship with vibraphonist Red Norvo and bassist Charles Mingus. The Red Norvo Trio, as they were called, produced a stream of best-selling records and became one of the most popular jazz acts of the 1950s. By this time, Farlow had developed an incredible technique, born out of the demands of working in such illustrious company—he was forced both to work hard on his solos and to provide a solid rhythm backing for the free-form excursions of Mingus and Norvo. Farlow had developed a style that involved creating lengthy melodic lines while incorporating the speed and dynamism characteristic of bebop, and was soon recognized as one of the best jazz guitar players in the world. Charlie Parker's rapid-fire saxophone playing and musical imagination were a major influence on Farlow's own style, and one of his earliest exercises was to learn Parker solos note for note—"It helps the development not to go for the easy stuff," he once commented, modestly. Farlow began recording under his own name and produced a series of fine albums for the Verve label, including *Autumn In New York* (1954), *The Tal Farlow Album* (1954), and *Tal* (1956).

Tal married in 1958 and moved to Sea Bright in New Jersey. There he resumed his old love of sign painting and, as a guitarist, began a long period of semiretirement, broken only by occasional periods of teaching guitar or sitting in at local jazz venues. He made brief musical comebacks in 1968 and 1975, and resumed his working relationship with Red Norvo when they played a world tour during the 1980s. A one-hour TV documentary made in 1981 and broadcast on both sides of the Atlantic, *Talmadge Farlow*, told his life story and revealed his incredible jazz guitar techniques to a wider audience, and he continued to play right through to the 1990s. Sadly, Farlow suffered from health problems during his later years and he died from esophageal cancer on July 25, 1998.

Tal Farlow, seen here in the mid-1950s, drew on bebop for his stunning technique, which was facilitated by his naturally large hands, enabling him to span large distances on the fretboard.

Lester Flatt

1914–1979

Lester Flatt was one of the most influential figures in bluegrass music. After serving as a guitarist and singer for mandolin virtuoso Bill Monroe (whose band, the Blue Grass Boys, gave the genre its name), he became coleader—with banjoist Earl Scruggs—of the Foggy Mountain Boys, who would eventually overtake even Monroe's ground-breaking ensemble in popularity and record sales.

Flatt, who hailed from Duncan's Chapel, Tennessee, was a former textile mill worker who began playing guitar in the 1930s, although he first came to fame as mandolinist and singer for the Kentucky Pardners, a group run by Bill Monroe's brother, Charlie, in 1943. Flatt switched to guitar after joining the Blue Grass Boys two years later (Earl Scruggs was hired soon afterward) and quickly made his mark in the band—supplying energetic rhythm parts on his big-bodied Martin acoustic, writing songs, and sharing lead vocals.

During this period, Flatt began to develop his "G run"—a trademark guitar figure marking the end of a solo break by one of his colleagues. The run started with a bass root note (typically a G, as this was a popular key for bluegrass numbers; the run could be transposed upward by using a capo), and ascended to the open third string (G) an octave above. The "G run" was widely copied and embellished by later players, and is now ubiquitous in bluegrass and other related styles.

In 1948, to Bill Monroe's fury, Flatt and Scruggs decided to leave the Blue Grass Boys; it would be decades before Monroe made peace with his two ex-bandmates. Shortly afterward, the duo formed the Foggy Mountain Boys, achieving rapid success with a repertoire that included "Foggy Mountain Breakdown" (1949)—used many years later on the film soundtrack to *Bonnie And Clyde* (1967). Other classic numbers showcased Earl's breathtaking banjo playing—fast, bluesy solos played using three fingers—and Lester's distinctive tenor voice. The duo toured extensively, undergoing several lineup changes, although Scruggs and Flatt remained throughout as group leaders. The Foggy Mountain Boys became regulars at Nashville's "Grand Ole Opry" and remained together until 1969, by which time musical differences made it impossible for the two to continue playing together. Scruggs wanted to experiment, Flatt preferred to stick with the original bluegrass acoustic approach.

After the band split, Flatt launched a new band, the Nashville Grass, and also recorded with singer (and former Foggy Mountain Boy) Mac Wiseman. He continued working throughout the 1970s despite a worsening heart condition that necessitated open-heart surgery in 1975. Flatt died in 1979; tantalizingly for fans of the famous duo, he had been discussing plans for a reunion with Scruggs in the months prior to his death.

Lester Flatt (left) and Earl Scruggs, shown here toward the end of their time together in the Foggy Mountain Boys, are probably country and western's most influential musical duo.

Jerry Garcia

1942–1995

Jerry Garcia first made a name for himself as a banjo and acoustic guitar picker in the area around his native San Francisco, playing bluegrass and jug band music before switching to electric guitar with The Warlocks—shortly to be renamed The Grateful Dead. In the mid-1960s, the group provided live music for author Ken Kesey's notorious Acid Tests, where their extended, improvisatory sets, with Garcia's alternately blistering and lyrical solo work well to the fore, formed an ideal soundtrack to the stoned antics of the participants.

This distinctive performing style became the Dead's artistic trademark, and they soon attracted a cult following that grew to extraordinary proportions and endured for decades. As their lead guitarist, principal songwriter (with lyricist Robert Hunter), and singer, Jerry Garcia was the focus of attention, affection, and reverence for many fans—although he remained profoundly uncomfortable with his gurulike status, seeing himself simply as a musician, not a spokesman or a sage.

Above: No guru, though looking every inch the part. Garcia onstage in 1982.

The Dead's full majesty, and much of Jerry's finest playing, is preserved on their live recordings; *Live Dead* (1969) is perhaps the best of these, capturing him at the peak of his instrumental prowess during the 23-minute "Dark Star." The band was frequently less successful at realizing its musical ambitions in the studio, but Garcia himself often excelled in this context. His economical, melodic solos and fills on the *Workingman's Dead* and *American Beauty* LPs (both 1970) give the lie to the accusations of aimless "noodling" sometimes leveled at him by detractors, and there are many other examples of powerful, driving guitar work on later Dead albums.

Garcia also had a busy musical life outside The Grateful Dead. He made several solo albums, appeared with the country-flavored New Riders of the Purple Sage (with whom he showcased his distinctive pedal steel guitar playing), and his own Jerry Garcia Band (which undertook a sell-out series of shows on New York's Broadway in 1991), and collaborated with bluegrass mandolinist David Grisman. He might have accomplished far more had it not been for the drug-related problems that dogged him constantly from the early 1980s onward, and were a major factor in his death at the age of only 53.

Left: Jerry Garcia onstage in the late 1960s. Over the years, the Grateful Dead drew on a melange of musical influences, aided by Garcia's catholic tastes and supreme musicianship.

Dave Gilmour

b.1944

Gilmour was brought up in the English city of Cambridge, where he developed an early interest in rock and roll. He started learning guitar at the age of 14, and was given a Fender Telecaster by his parents for his 21st birthday. At around this time, his band, Jokers Wild, appeared at a local party with The Pink Floyd Sound, a group that featured Cambridge-born singer and guitarist Syd Barrett. By the summer of 1967, Pink Floyd (as they were now known) had produced two hit singles and a best-selling album, *The Piper At The Gates Of Dawn*, and was regarded as England's prime psychedelic group. Unfortunately, Barrett's mental state was deteriorating alarmingly during this period, due in part to his consumption of LSD, and in early 1968 Gilmour was asked to take over the ailing musician's vocal and instrumental duties. The group initially attempted to continue as a quintet, with Barrett in the role of a nonperforming songwriter, but this proved to be unworkable due to his increasingly fragile state of mind. Gilmour became Floyd's sole guitarist after Barrett was asked to leave that April.

Gilmour's playing and songwriting brought a warm, humanizing element to Pink Floyd's increasingly elaborate, painstakingly assembled, and sometimes highly contrived work in the studio and onstage. His contribution to "One Of These Days" (1971), featuring slide parts played on an electric lap steel guitar, counterbalanced the track's repetitious bass lines and processed vocals. The classic "Money" from *Dark Side Of The Moon* (1973) was made instantly memorable by its cash-register effects, but owed much of its impact to Gilmour's tremolo-laden chords and powerful solo. On "Shine On You Crazy Diamond" (a touching tribute to Barrett) and "Wish You Were Here" (1975), his superbly controlled note-bending and rich guitar sounds (from bell-like Stratocaster to delicate acoustic) dominated the lush production.

During the late 1970s, Gilmour was increasingly involved in personal projects, helping to launch the career of singer Kate Bush, and releasing his own first solo LP in 1978. However, he remained strongly committed to Pink Floyd, despite growing tensions between himself and bassist Roger Waters following the completion of *The Wall* (1979). Extracted from the album, "Another Brick In The Wall" gave Pink Floyd their first U.K. and U.S. number 1. The song's lengthy coda featured a classic Gilmour solo, characterized by bluesy string-bending and soaring, sustained notes. Waters left the band in 1985, and after some complex legal maneuvering, Gilmour subsequently became their new leader. Pink Floyd continues to record and perform together (the band issued a live double CD, *Pulse*, in 1995) while Gilmour also undertakes occasional solo appearances, often in the company of other leading rock names such as Pete Townshend and John Entwistle.

Dave Gilmour's blues-derived guitar playing did much to make Pink Floyd's often bleak sound more accessible. He is seen here onstage in the 1970s.

Freddie Green

1911–1987

While most jazz guitar legends made their names as virtuoso soloists of the instrument, Freddie Green's reputation grew entirely out of his prowess as a brilliant accompanist. For more than 50 years, his phenomenal rhythm guitar playing was the backbone of one of the greatest rhythm sections in history, that of the dynamically extrovert Count Basie Orchestra, and served as an inspiration to many other musicians.

Freddie Green was born in Charleston, South Carolina on March 31, 1911. He showed an early interest in music and started playing the banjo and guitar at the age of 10. After the death of his parents, Green moved to New York to live with his aunt and by the time he was 16, he was making a living as an upholsterer during the day and a guitar player by night. John Hammond, a successful record producer, heard Green perform at the Black Cat in Greenwich Village in 1937 and recommended him to Count Basie, who was looking for a replacement for the recently departed guitarist Claude Williams. After an audition in Basie's dressing room at the Roseland Ballroom, the bandleader took Green on; the two were to continue working together until Basie's death in 1984.

After Charlie Christian, the guitar was increasingly regarded as a solo instrument in jazz, a contrast to its use during the Big Band era as an accompaniment to help keep time. Green, however, rarely played solo notes with Basie's orchestra, preferring instead to focus on his now-celebrated rhythm playing. Although he played on each beat of the bar, and was never ostentatious, his light, driving strumming became an integral part of Basie's rhythm section. Trumpeter and arranger Buck Clayton has noted that Basie did not play much with his left hand and that Green compensated for this rhythmical and bass deficiency with his guitar playing. As a composer, he wrote "Down for Double," "Right On," and "Corner Pocket" for Basie's orchestra. Green played on virtually all of the Basie albums, including *Count Basie Swings—Joe Williams Sings* (1955), *The Swinging Count* (1955), *The Atomic Mr. Basie* (1957), *The Count Basie Story* (1961), *Count Basie And The Kansas City Seven* (1962), and *At The Montreux Jazz Festival* (1975). He used only a single microphone, never an amplifier, yet Green can be heard clearly on the recordings.

Freddie Green was one of the most sought-after jazz rhythm guitarists from the late 1930s through to the mid-1980s. During this period he worked with many of the most celebrated names in jazz, including Benny Goodman, Lionel Hampton, Lester Young, Teddy Wilson, Benny Carter, and Buck Clayton. He even played guitar with the Count Basie Orchestra after their leader's death, and his final recording with them featured on *Diane Schuur And The Count Basie Orchestra* (1987), an album that has since been dedicated to him. He died in Las Vegas on March 1, 1987.

Freddie Green, seen here in a recording studio during the 1940s, reestablished the role of the guitar as a rhythmical accompaniment in jazz through his work with Count Basie.

Peter Green

b.1946

Born and brought up in the East End of London, Peter Green was given his first guitar lessons by his brother, developed a fascination with R&B and the blues (especially as played by B.B. King) as a teenager, and began his musical career while also working in a butcher's shop near his home. His potential was quickly spotted by Bluesbreakers bandleader John Mayall, who used Green as a replacement for his regular lead guitarist, Eric Clapton, in 1965 (during Clapton's temporary absence in Greece). Mayall gave him a permanent job with the group the following year, when Clapton departed to form Cream.

As a Bluesbreaker, Green worked alongside bassist John McVie and, later, drummer Mick Fleetwood. However, in the summer of 1967, Fleetwood and Green left Mayall's band to form the first incarnation of Fleetwood Mac, together with a brilliant young slide guitarist, Jeremy Spencer, a devotee of Elmore James. A stand-in bassist, Bob Brunning, was replaced by John McVie that fall.

Brunning describes Green's guitar playing during those years as "sparse, emotive [and] liquid," and such qualities are all clearly apparent on Fleetwood Mac's early records. These include the original version of "Black Magic Woman" (1968), composed by Green and later a hit for Carlos Santana, and "Albatross,"a moody, atmospheric instrumental that topped the U.K. singles charts in January 1969. Sadly, though, Fleetwood Mac's success soon began to take its toll. Business difficulties plagued the band in 1969, and were followed by signs that Peter Green was suffering from mental problems, exacerbated by his use of LSD. In particular, the guitarist was starting to feel increasingly uncomfortable about the large amounts of money he was now earning. Initially he channeled this angst into making some truly marvelous music. The ambitious "Oh Well," featured a cynical lyric, a driving acoustic riff married to shrieking lead guitar, and a lengthy, flamenco-influenced coda; "The Green Manalishi (With The Two-Prong Crown)," a dark piece featuring edgy, abrasive guitar and eerie vocals over the fade-out, was an unsettling reflection of Green's mental state. Green left the group in summer 1970 (returning briefly in 1971 to help them complete a U.S. tour after Jeremy Spencer left to join a religious cult). Thereafter, he released a prophetically titled solo LP, *The End Of The Game* (1970), and began a lengthy period of absence from professional playing.

Over the following years, Green made sporadic reappearances on the music scene, but his real comeback came in 1996, when he launched his Splinter Group, a highly acclaimed blues-rock band, the original lineup of which featured heavy rock bassist Neil Murray and drummer Cozy Powell. The band has toured extensively, and issued several albums, including the all-acoustic *Robert Johnson Songbook* (1998) and *Clown* (2001).

Peter Green onstage with Fleetwood Mac in the late 1960s. Green's clean, economical playing made him an emotive interpreter of the blues, a genre to which he has returned in later life.

Buddy Guy

Born in Lettsworth, Louisiana, Buddy Guy taught himself to play guitar on a homemade instrument by listening to records on the radio. He served a brief musical apprenticeship in his home state, jamming with local musicians including Slim Harpo and Lightin' Slim, before moving to Chicago in 1957. Within a year of his arrival, he had won a "Battle of the Blues" contest at the city's celebrated Blue Flame Club, and had begun recording for the Artistic label. The company later went bankrupt, but soon afterward Guy was introduced to Chess Records by blues great Willie Dixon. He quickly signed a new deal with the company and became a member of the Chess houseband, going on to appear on releases by Muddy Waters and Howlin' Wolf.

Guy launched his own prolific seven-year solo career at Chess with a powerful debut single, "First Time I Met the Blues" (1960). This song goes for the jugular, like many of Guy's finest tracks. The flurries of notes and vibrato-laden chords from his guitar are matched in intensity by his impassioned vocal, and the mood of tension and immediacy leaps out at the listener. Buddy is just as impressive on more reflective numbers such as "My Time After Awhile" (1964), with its subtle interplay between horns and guitar. By the mid-1960s, Guy's work for Chess was displaying a strong soul influence, earning him the displeasure of some diehard blues critics. But Guy was already winning a host of new fans for his live appearances, during which he would readily indulge in acts of showmanship, such as wandering into the audience while still playing.

Soon, Guy and his regular onstage partner, harmonica player Junior Wells, were attracting the attention of performers such as The Rolling Stones (with whom Guy and Wells toured in 1970) and Eric Clapton, who coproduced their album *Buddy Guy And Junior Wells Play The Blues* (1972). But Guy's consistent live popularity was not matched by the size or quality of his studio output during the 1970s and 1980s. The appearance of *Damn Right, I've Got The Blues* in 1991 served as a timely reminder of his enduring importance—and his ability to attract star collaborators. The Grammy-winning album featured guest appearances by Clapton (who had invited Guy onstage with him at London's Royal Albert Hall in the early 1990s), Jeff Beck, and Mark Knopfler. The set included "Rememberin' Stevie," a touching tribute to another of Buddy's admirers, Stevie Ray Vaughan, who had died the previous year.

Guy maintained his high profile throughout the 1990s and into the 21st century. *Feels Like Rain* (1993), his follow-up to *Damn Right I've Got The Blues*, was also awarded a Grammy. His subsequent releases include *Live: The Real Deal* (1996), which captures Guy in full flight during concerts in New York and at his own Chicago club, Legends.

Burning it up live. Buddy Guy's showmanship, as well as his ability to produce frenetic, wailing blues solos, was a major influence on Jimi Hendrix.

Jim Hall

b.1930

Jim Hall is one of the most respected jazz guitar players in the world. Unlike most virtuosos, he doesn't often play a plethora of notes in his solos. Hall's approach has always been to play thoughtful, lyrical passages with a depth and subtlety that few other musicians have been able to achieve. His style, which first came to prominence in the 1950s, was a major influence on younger players such as Pat Metheny, John Scofield, and John McLaughlin.

Jim Hall was born in Buffalo, New York, on December 4, 1930. As a child he was surrounded by music—his grandfather was a violinist and his mother played the piano. However, it was his uncle, a guitar player, who influenced young Jim to take up the six-stringed instrument at the age of 10. His talent soon became apparent and by the time he was 13 he was playing professionally in local dance bands. The Hall family moved over to Cleveland, Ohio, in 1946. A clarinet player in a band that Hall joined there directed his attention to Benny Goodman's "Solo Flight," featuring Charlie Christian. The guitarist made an immediate impression on Hall: "It was instant addiction," he recalls. Later, he discovered Django Reinhardt, who quickly became another major early influence. Hall moved to Los Angeles in 1955 to study music at UCLA and classical guitar with Vicente Gomez. A brief spell with Chico Hamilton's jazz band raised Hall's profile as an accompanist and, by the late 1950s, the young guitarist found himself working with Ella Fitzgerald and Yves Montand. By this time, Hall had developed his own distinctively lyrical playing style, characterized by a bluesy swing coupled with a delicate touch.

A refreshing receptiveness to new influences has been a characteristic of Jim Hall's career since its earliest days. For example, after completing a tour of South America with Ella Fitzgerald in the late 1950s, Hall decided to stay behind to soak up some Latin-American musical flavors. Bossa nova was in its infancy at the time, and Hall swiftly picked up on the new form, later incorporating elements of it into his work with Sonny Rollins (*What's New*, 1962) and his two 1963 albums with Paul Desmond (*Take Ten* and *Bossa Antigua*).

Hall moved to New York in 1960 and worked as a studio musician on Merv Griffin's popular TV show. He also started working with other top jazzers, including pianist George Shearing, bass player Ron Carter, saxophonist Ornette Coleman, and trumpeter Chet Baker. Since then he has made several recordings under his own name, including *Intermodulation* (1966), *Live In Tokyo* (1976), *Jim Hall's Three* (1986), and *Subsequently* (1992). His desire to experiment has not diminished with age. In 1996 he told *Just Jazz Guitar* magazine, "My playing has changed and I hope it continues to change—not because you want to throw away your values, but because you want to keep growing all the time." He was awarded the prestigious Jazzpar Prize in Copenhagen on April 5, 1998.

Jim Hall's mellow touch makes for a highly expressive form of jazz guitar, one in which feeling rather than technical wizardry is the main criterion. He is shown here in 1958.

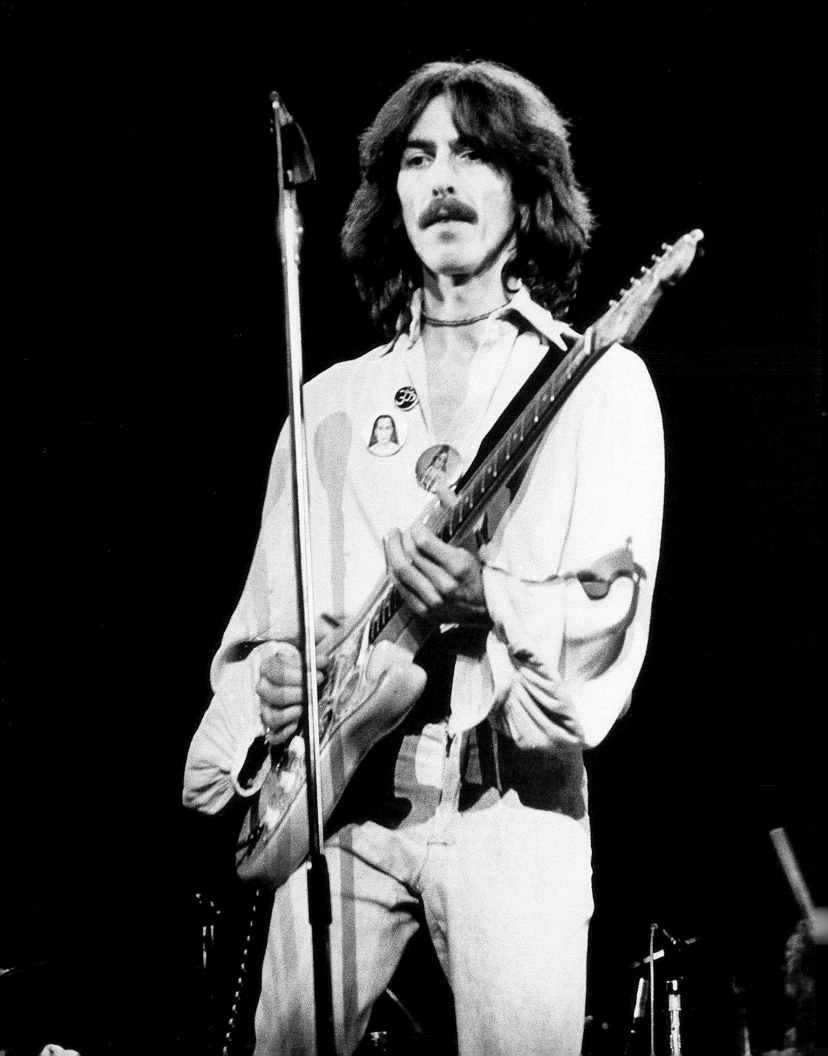

George Harrison

b.1943

George Harrison decided to learn guitar after hearing Lonnie Donegan's version of Leadbelly's "Rock Island Line" in 1956. While mastering the basics of the instrument, Harrison developed a strong interest in rockabilly, and a special admiration for Carl Perkins, who was to become one of his most enduring musical influences.

In 1958, George joined fellow Liverpudlians John Lennon and Paul McCartney in the Quarrymen—the skiffle group that evolved into The Beatles. They put in years of arduous live work before their first chart successes in 1962–3, becoming a tight, highly disciplined unit whose songs had no space for overplaying or grandstanding. Harrison's solos were therefore usually brief and carefully integrated into a song, making him more of an ensemble player than a virtuoso. His riffing was the driving force behind numbers such as "Day Tripper" (1965) and "Paperback Writer" (1966); and sometimes, his choice of instrument and sound—electric 12-string on "A Hard Day's Night," Spanish guitar for "And I Love Her" (both 1964)—was almost as important as the notes he played.

During The Beatles' later years, Harrison's musical adventurousness and composing ability grew steadily, and he amassed a large backlog of material for which there was no outlet within the group. Much of this was showcased on his first post-Beatles project, the highly acclaimed triple LP *All Things Must Pass* (1970). Eric Clapton and Ringo Starr were among the rock luminaries guesting on the album, for which Bob Dylan also provided two songs, one—"I'd Have You Anytime"—co-written with George. Many of the album's contributors reunited onstage with Harrison in 1971 for two fund-raising concerts at New York's Madison Square Garden. Harrison organized the concerts to raise funds for the victims of famine and war in Bangladesh, prompted by a plea from friend Ravi Shankar, with whom Harrison had studied sitar in the mid-1960s.

Living In the Material World (1973) topped the U.S. album charts and made number 2 in the U.K., but some of Harrison's subsequent solo records were less well received, especially in Britain. However, in the 1980s he began a fruitful collaboration with ex-ELO leader Jeff Lynne, who co-produced the album *Cloud Nine* (1988), an unexpected commercial triumph for Harrison, reaching the Top 10 on both sides of the Atlantic and giving him a U.S. chart-topper with the single "Got My Mind Set On You." Lynne also produced the Traveling Wilburys' albums (the other Wilburys were Lynne, Bob Dylan, Tom Petty, and Roy Orbison) whose first hit, "Handle With Care," featured a vocal from Harrison.

George Harrison's accomplishments with The Beatles, in which his talent and enthusiasm for the guitar played a pivotal role, gave an important boost to the instrument's profile and encouraged countless new players to take it up—achievements that are his lasting legacy.

George Harrison's economical guitar playing was vital to The Beatles' sound, a refreshing contrast to the overindulgence of many rock guitarists. He is shown here onstage in 1974.

Jimi Hendrix

1942–1970

Jimi Hendrix's work as a journeyman guitarist in the early 1960s, backing artists such as the Isley Brothers and Wilson Pickett, gave little hint of his true abilities, which only began to emerge after his arrival in New York in 1964. Two years later, British musician Chas Chandler, who had heard Jimi at a club gig in Greenwich Village, brought him to London and teamed him with bassist Noel Redding and drummer Mitch Mitchell, creating The Jimi Hendrix Experience.

Hendrix's impact on the music scene was swift and profound, and his guitar work was nothing short of revolutionary. A left-hander, he coaxed an extraordinary range of sounds from his reverse-strung right-handed Fender Stratocaster. Many such sounds were already in evidence on his debut LP, *Are You Experienced?* (1967): skillfully controlled feedback, distinctive use of wah-wah and vibrato, and a stylistic approach that reflected his love of blues and jazz, while also prefiguring many future developments in hard rock.

Above: Jimi Hendrix on the brink of his breakthrough in London, 1967.

In June 1967, the Experience made their U.S. debut at the Monterey Pop Festival, where Hendrix concluded a powerful performance by setting fire to his guitar. Other major concerts followed, and the release of a new LP, *Axis: Bold As Love*, at the end of the year, further boosted his reputation. However, the album—recorded just after *Are You Experienced?*—did not represent Jimi's latest musical ideas, which found fuller expression on *Electric Ladyland* (1968), with its imaginative use of studio electronics. The LP included the classic "Voodoo Chile (Slight Return)" and a version of Bob Dylan's "All Along The Watchtower" that eclipsed the original.

Electric Ladyland was to be the Experience's swan song. Four months after appearing at the Woodstock Festival in August 1969, where he delivered what critic Stephanie Zacharek memorably described as a "bruised, fractured, and beautiful" rendition of "The Star-Spangled Banner," Jimi launched his Band of Gypsies with drummer Buddy Miles and bassist Billy Cox. Miles was subsequently replaced by Mitch Mitchell, and it was he and Cox who accompanied the guitarist's often erratic final performances. On September 18, 1970, Jimi Hendrix died in London after taking an overdose of sleeping pills, vomiting in his sleep and suffocating—a tawdry end to an awesome talent.

Left: Near the end of his career, Jimi performed a ragged set at the Isle of Wight Festival, in August 1970. Within a month he would be dead.

Allan Holdsworth

b.1946

There are few musicians, let alone guitar players, with a style as original and distinctive as that of Allan Holdsworth. Contemporary musicians view him as an uncompromising virtuoso who expanded the range of the electric guitar, although jazz and rock audiences still know little about him. His style is characterized by spectacular chord voicings and enigmatic melodies. Although many of Holdsworth's solos feature extraordinarily complicated lead lines, the playing exudes a warmth and depth of expression that is often missing in that of other technically outstanding guitar players.

Allan Holdsworth was born in Bradford, England. As a child he received music lessons from his father Sam, a gifted amateur musician, but it was the jazz sounds of Charlie Parker and Django Reinhardt that inspired him to take up music seriously. Holdsworth started playing the guitar during his late teens, gigging around the pub circuit in northern England, and quickly evolving into an original and virtuosic instrumentalist. His distinctive sound reached the ears of ex-Miles Davis drummer Tony Williams, who promptly signed him up for his 1975 recording, *Believe It*. Holdsworth's guitar was prominent on the album and it made a big impression on the jazz-rock scene: he immediately became one of the most sought-after players in the genre. After his work with Williams, Holdsworth collaborated with experimental Anglo-French progressive rockers Gong and played on a number of seminal fusion albums including Soft Machine's *Bundles* (1975) and Jean-Luc Ponty's *Enigmatic Ocean* (1977). His smooth, legato lead approach, contrasting markedly with the heavily picked styles of Al Di Meola and John McLaughlin, was a major influence on younger rock and jazz players. In 1980, Holdsworth formed the I.O.U. band (named after the group's financial status) with drummer Gary Husband and bassist Paul Carmichael. However, the group recorded only one album, *Allan Holdsworth, I.O.U.* (1982), before promptly disbanding. From the mid-1980s, Holdsworth established himself as a pioneer of the SynthAxe, a guitarlike synthesizer featuring a breath controller, which enabled him to introduce effects such as tremolo or vibrato to his note playing. Holdsworth had been fascinated by the saxophone as a young man, and the SynthAxe enabled him to combine his skills as a guitarist with a means of note production more usually associated with brass and wind instruments.

Disillusioned with the lack of interest from the British music scene, Holdsworth emigrated to California in 1982, and has lived there ever since. Over the years he has recorded a number of critically acclaimed but commercially unsuccessful albums, including *Secrets* (1989) and *The Sixteen Men Of Tain* (2000). Allan Holdsworth remains an archetypal musician's musician.

Little known to the general music public, Allan Holdsworth is revered by fellow guitarists for his highly innovative, jazz-influenced guitar playing. He is shown here onstage in London in 1979.

Sol Hoopii

Solomon Ho'opi'i Ka'ai'ai—who simplified his stage name to Sol Hoopii—is recognized today as one of the greatest players of the Hawaiian, or steel, guitar. This instrument, held horizontally on the lap and fretted with a steel bar, originated in Hawaii during the 1880s, and became popular on the U.S. mainland after musicians from the islands were featured at San Francisco's Panama Pacific Exhibition in 1915. Soon, the U.S. was in the grip of an Hawaiian guitar craze, and four years later, the booming demand for players persuaded the 17-year-old Sol (who had been an expert on the instrument since childhood) to leave his home in Honolulu and stow away onboard a San Francisco-bound ocean liner.

Hoopii was to have a highly successful American career. After moving to Los Angeles, he quickly became a star attraction at smart nightclubs and restaurants, playing in a trio with Lani McIntire and Glenwood Leslie. His initial musical forays were made on an acoustic guitar, but it was on the new electric Rickenbacker guitars that he began to make his name as a steel guitarist.

Hoopii made his first records in 1925, and by the end of the decade his reputation as a virtuoso had spread across the U.S. His style was characterized by agile fretting with the steel bar and rapid, powerful hand picking. It was not just the speed and precision of his technique that made him stand out, however, but also his ability to absorb a wide range of styles. Hoopii's repertoire included rags, blues, and the latest jazz tunes, and he combined traditional Hawaiian sounds with contemporary musical influences in numbers such as his best-selling "Hula Blues." His popularity extended to that of his instrument of choice, a National Reso-Phonic, the sales of which rose considerably during his heyday.

During the 1930s, Hoopii began to appear in Hollywood movies, playing onscreen in *Bird of Paradise* (1932), *Flirtation Walk* (1934), Bing Crosby's *Waikiki Wedding* (1937), and *Song Of The Islands* (1942), as well as performing on the soundtracks of the Charlie Chan film series. He was also in heavy demand as a live performer, and continued to record extensively. However, in 1938, he decided to devote himself to Aimee Semple McPherson's International Church of the Foursquare Gospel, and became a traveling evangelist. Most of his subsequent music had a religious flavor, though it retained its former brilliance. On one of Sol's later recordings, "Train Song (Life's Railway To Heaven)," he even managed to coax engine whistles and animal noises out of his electric steel guitar!

Sol Hoopii returned to Hawaii for a tour in 1948 and remained active in the studio until 1951. He died from diabetes in Seattle on November 16, 1953, having made his final concert appearance there a few months earlier.

Sol Hoopii was the first major star of the Hawaiian guitar. He is shown here in 1951, holding a Serenader steel guitar made by Bud Tutmarc. The instrument's slanted pickup enabled a guitarist to obtain a much richer bass sound.

Elmore James

1918–1963

Elmore James was a key transitional figure in blues history. Starting out as an acoustic guitarist, he had switched to electric guitar by the mid-1940s, specializing in searing slide playing. James was one of the wave of Mississippi Delta bluesmen who later found fame in Chicago, creating a potent new urban strain of the music there.

Born in Richland, Mississippi, James's first "instrument" consisted of a tin can, a wooden board, and a single metal string; he subsequently graduated to a cheap acoustic guitar. By 1937, James had met the legendary Robert Johnson, then appearing throughout the Delta with harmonica player and singer Rice Miller (a.k.a. Sonny Boy Williamson II). Miller was to become one of James's closest musical associates, but it was from Robert Johnson that the young guitarist picked up the song he would later make his own: "I Believe I'll Dust My Broom," with its distinctive triplet riff.

Following Johnson's death in 1938, James occasionally guested on Miller's "King Biscuit Time" radio show. After war service in the U.S. Navy, he returned to Mississippi, reunited with Miller, and started to develop a more powerful sound, playing electric slide guitar with one of the first electric blues bands in the Delta. In 1952, when James's recording of "Dust My Broom" (with Miller on harmonica) reached number 9 in the national R&B charts, he capitalized on his success by moving to Chicago, dividing most of his later career between the Windy City and the Delta.

Other Mississippi-born blues artists were already established in Chicago by the 1950s, but Elmore James's group, The Broomdusters, soon won the accolade of "the hottest band in town." Elmore himself was a passionate singer and an exciting, if limited, guitarist. He managed to work the "Dust My Broom" riff into the majority of his songs, most obviously on "Wild About You Baby," "I Believe," and "Dust My Blues." James recorded initially for Chicago's Meteor records, though he subsequently also laid down tracks for the Chief and Chess labels. His scorching impact, however, is preserved at its most intense on the tracks he recorded for the Fire label from 1959 onward. These include frequently covered classics such as "Shake Your Money Maker" (later reworked by Peter Green's Fleetwood Mac), "The Sky Is Crying," and "Look On Yonder Wall."

Elmore James's early death, from heart trouble, took place in Chicago on May 24, 1963. Hampered by his inability to sustain a long-term recording contract, and possibly by the repetitive quality of his material, his music had remained largely unknown outside the Delta and Chicago during his lifetime. Only a few years later, young white musicians such as Eric Clapton, Peter Green, and Duane Allman were to reawaken interest in electric Chicago blues, name checking James as a pioneering influence.

Elmore James was one of the most important guitarists of the postwar period. His fiery slide guitar playing became a major influence on the evolution of electric blues.

Bert Jansch

b.1943

Although not as well known internationally as many guitar icons, Bert Jansch has influenced generations of aspiring guitarists. Born in Scotland, he took up the acoustic guitar in his teens, dropping out of school to pursue his fascination with the instrument. Jansch hitchhiked to London from his native Edinburgh in the early 1960s, and emerged as a prominent figure on the folk scene there, performing in tiny clubs such as the Troubadour in Earl's Court (where the young Bob Dylan once did a floor spot), and alongside artists including Donovan, Stefan Grossman, and Davy Graham at Les Cousins in Soho.

Jansch subsequently covered Graham's popular instrumental "Angi," on his eponymous debut LP, released in 1965. This reworked version, which was to become better known than Graham's original, contained the seeds of the so-called "folk-baroque" style that Bert was soon to refine and popularize. Unlike the dull, inert guitar parts favored by some earlier folkies, Jansch's playing—whether accompanying his own idiosyncratic vocals, or on solo instrumental numbers—was distinguished by rhythmic intensity and rich, often elaborately decorated melodic textures. He was admired and emulated far beyond his immediate musical circle; leading rock names who drew on his ideas included Jimmy Page, whose "Black Mountain Side" (*Led Zeppelin*, 1969) was inspired by Bert's memorable arrangement of the folk song "Blackwaterside" (1966). Neil Young once commented, "As much of a great guitar player as Jimi [Hendrix] was, Bert Jansch is the same thing for acoustic guitar … and my favorite."

In 1967, Jansch and fellow guitarist John Renbourn formed Pentangle with vocalist Jacqui McShee, string bassist Danny Thompson, and drummer Terry Cox. The group enjoyed considerable popularity in Britain and the U.S., and had minor U.K. hit singles with "Once I Had A Sweetheart" (1969) and "Light Flight" (1970). Pentangle toured extensively during the late 1960s and early 1970s, headlining at prestigious venues such as London's Royal Albert Hall and the Carnegie Hall in New York. After the group split up in 1973, Jansch made a succession of solo LPs, including *L.A. Turnaround* (1974), produced by ex-Monkee Mike Nesmith; however, the following years brought him only mixed artistic and commercial success, and were complicated by financial difficulties and problems with alcohol.

More recently, Jansch's career has undergone a considerable resurgence, and his influence has been acknowledged by a new generation of guitarists, among them established names such as Oasis's Noel Gallagher, Johnny Marr, and ex-Suede star Bernard Butler. Marr and Butler both contributed to Jansch's highly acclaimed CD *Crimson Moon* (2000), which also features Jansch's son Adam on bass.

A youthful Bert Jansch. Although best-known as a folk guitarist, Jansch's role in the course of rock music, via his influence on musicians such as Jimmy Page, Neil Young, and Johnny Marr, is incalculable.

Lonnie Johnson

1889–1970

Lonnie Johnson was a highly influential blues pioneer and jazz guitar player. His first recordings, made during the 1920s and 1930s, inspired Charlie Christian, Django Reinhardt, and many other guitarists to play blues and jazz.

Alonzo "Lonnie" Johnson was born in New Orleans, Louisiana on February 8, 1889, and as a child he learned the guitar, violin, and piano. By the early 1900s he was playing guitar in Louisiana cafés and saloons with his brother James "Steady Roll" Johnson. In 1917, he traveled to Europe to play there but returned to find that a flu epidemic had killed most of his relatives. He moved to St. Louis in 1922 and won a blues contest there in 1925. Okeh Records, who organized the contest, signed Johnson up and he became a regular member of their house band, playing with a number of prominent blues and jazz artists, including Louis Armstrong and Duke Ellington. However, his most celebrated recordings were made with another jazz guitarist, Eddie Lang (who went under the pseudonym of Blind Willie Dunn when performing blues). Johnson played with a more sophisticated touch than many of his blues peers, injecting a rhythmical swing into his songs and drawing on a broad base of chord variations. By contrast, his lyrics were often stark and hard-hitting.

Above: For much of his long performing career, Lonnie Johnson played only acoustic guitars.

In 1932, Johnson moved to Cleveland, where he worked in factories by day and did sessions, live performances, and radio shows by night. He started to play an amplified guitar during the 1940s and his music began to grow a little in popularity; one of his singles, "Confused" (1950), made the R&B charts. However, Johnson could not make a steady living as a musician and he was forced to work for a while as a chef in Philadelphia during the late 1950s. Things had picked up by the early 1960s, however, and he was soon playing with Duke Ellington in New York, touring with a blues package in Europe, and recording his own album, *Tomorrow Night* (1963). He settled in Toronto, Canada, during the late 1960s and remained there until he died from a heart attack on June 16, 1970.

Left: A study of quiet elegance. Lonnie Johnson brought an urbane touch to his playing of six- and 12-string guitars. He favored single-string solos, often employing a dramatic vibrato, and drew on a relatively advanced knowledge of chord variations and harmony.

Robert Johnson

1911–1938

Robert Johnson brought a startling new intensity to the Mississippi Delta blues, often supporting his tortured vocals with biting slide work, and creating compelling, driving accompaniments that seem far beyond the capabilities of a single acoustic guitar. There has long been speculation over how Johnson acquired his formidable performing skills. He showed little early promise as a guitarist, seeming destined for life as a plantation worker in the Delta town of Robinsonville until 1930, when the death in childbirth of his 16-year-old wife, Virginia, precipitated his departure from the area. Returning to his birthplace, Hazlehurst (about 200 miles to the south), Johnson remarried and began to work seriously on his playing. This developed so remarkably during the year or more he spent away from the Delta that he was suspected of achieving his musical skills by selling his soul to the Devil.

In fact, Johnson's prowess required no supernatural explanation. Supported by his new wife, he was able to devote himself entirely to music, sitting in with performers at juke-joints and dances, listening avidly to records and radio, and constantly expanding his repertoire of songs and licks. His slide guitar playing was doubtless influenced by blues greats Son House, Willie Brown, and Charley Patton, all of whom the young Johnson saw perform at picnics and dances in the Mississippi Delta. Yet in many ways the story of a satanic pact seems disturbingly appropriate. After leaving Hazlehurst, Johnson was rarely short of work as a musician, but the rootless, nightmarish quality of his subsequent life is vividly documented in his song lyrics, some of which ("Hellhound On My Trail," "Me And the Devil Blues") contain chilling images of possession and pursuit. The circumstances of his early death (from pneumonia after being poisoned by a jealous husband) added further to the stock of rumor and superstition surrounding his star-crossed career.

Remarkably, Johnson's towering reputation as a blues guitarist rests on only a handful of recordings. His first recording session, which took place in November 1936 in a hotel room in San Antonio, Texas, yielded 16 tracks, including "I Believe I'll Dust My Broom," "Crossroad Blues," and "Terraplane Blues." A second session, which took place in a Dallas warehouse in June 1937, produced "Love In Vain Blues" and "Hellhound On My Trail," among others. Johnson recorded 29 tracks in all, changing the history of the blues and, by implication, popular music in the process.

A handful of Johnson's songs remained popular with his contemporaries, but it was not until the 1960s, when his music was championed by several young blues-inspired rock players, notably Eric Clapton and Keith Richards, that he achieved wider recognition. He is now regarded as one of the greatest of all prewar blues artists, and his reissued recordings have become million sellers.

A dapper Robert Johnson, photographed shortly before his untimely death. Johnson's extraordinarily dextrous playing was facilitated by his large hands and long fingers.

Barney Kessel

b.1923

Barney Kessel was born in Muskogee, Oklahoma on October 17, 1923. He started playing guitar at the age of 12 and within a couple of years was playing in a local jazz orchestra. While he was still a teenager, Kessel met guitar legend Charlie Christian by chance in an Oklahoma City nightclub. Impressed by the youngster's talent, Christian offered to pass his name on to renowned bandleader Benny Goodman. Christian's guitar playing was a great influence on Kessel's playing, which was essentially a further refinement of the older guitarist's style. Kessel worked hard on his technique to create his own exciting, "straight-ahead" bebop jazz guitar, with no blues licks.

Although he soon became well known locally as a talented guitarist, Kessel realized that there wasn't a career for a jazz musician in Muskogee, and he moved to Los Angeles in 1942. Life wasn't easy there and, at first, he had to make a living out of washing dishes at a restaurant, but he managed to get a break with the Chico Marx (of Marx Brothers fame) Orchestra in 1943, and this led to radio and studio work. A year later he appeared as the only white musician in an award-winning documentary film, *Jammin' The Blues*. Word of Kessel's abilities soon spread and during the remainder of the decade he also played with the bands of Artie Shaw, Charlie Barnet, and eventually Benny Goodman himself.

Kessel's reputation as a first-class guitarist grew during the 1950s and he recorded a series of albums that took jazz guitar playing to another level: *Easy Like* (1953), *To Swing Or Not To Swing* (1955), *Sessions, Live* (1956), and *Let's Cook* (1957). He played guitar on Billie Holiday's *Body And Soul* (1957) and Julie London's classic "Cry Me A River" (1955), and worked with the Oscar Peterson Trio. However, as an in-demand session musician in his heyday, Kessel also worked on many nonjazz-related projects, including recordings by Ricky Nelson in the 1950s and 1960s and several Elvis Presley film soundtracks. He continued into and through the 1960s with *Workin' Out* (1961), *On Fire* (1965), *Swingin' Easy* (1968), and *Kessel's Kit* (1969). By the 1970s he was a jazz superstar and teamed up with fellow guitarists Herb Ellis and Charlie Byrd to form Great Guitars, one of the most celebrated guitar collaborations of all time. Their 1970s recordings, including *Great Guitars: Straight Tracks* (1978) and *Great Guitars At The Winery* (1980), are considered by many aficionados to be milestones in jazz guitar history. He later recorded *Spontaneous Combustion* (1987) with the Jamaican-born pianist, Monty Alexander.

Kessel has also been a respected music educator for the past 20 years. He wrote a regular jazz tuition column in *Guitar Player* magazine during the 1980s and also produced several instruction videos for guitar players. He was forced to give up playing after a major stroke in 1992, but still continues to teach selected pupils.

Barney Kessel's guitar playing was rooted in the bebop of Charlie Christian. Kessel is shown here taking a break between sets during a live appearance in the mid-1940s.

Albert King

1923–1992

Albert King was the only guitarist of his generation to succeed in combining the blues with the soul sounds of the 1960s and 1970s. His recordings for the Stax label during this period brought him hits and extensive airplay, delighted black and white audiences, and made him a leading live attraction—while retaining the gritty integrity of the style he had spent so many years honing on the club circuit.

King was born Albert Nelson in Indianola, Mississippi. In about 1931, his family moved north to Forrest City, Arkansas, where Albert began to teach himself guitar on a homemade instrument. A left-hander, he used standard guitars "upside down," with the treble strings farthest from the floor, developing a highly individual technique to cope with this inverted set-up. Rather than working on flashy showmanship, King strove to capture a soulful intensity in his solos, which were often played on only one string. In particular, he developed a technique of note bending that resulted in a distinctive howl. King spent much of his early career playing small venues in the riverside town of Osceola (also working in Indiana and Chicago, where he adopted the name King), before settling in St. Louis in 1956. There, he had an R&B Top 20 hit with "Don't Throw Your Love On Me So Strong" (1961), although sustained commercial success was to elude him until he joined Stax in Memphis, five years later.

At Stax, King's husky vocals, punctuated by terse, stinging outbursts from "Lucy," his Gibson Flying V, were combined, to superb effect, with backing from Stax house band Booker T. and the MGs. Best-selling records such as "Laundromat Blues," "Crosscut Saw" (both 1966), and "Born Under A Bad Sign" (1967) led to appearances alongside major rock acts at big venues and festivals; indeed, he became the first blues artist to play at San Francisco's Fillmore West, appearing on the debut bill alongside John Mayall and Jimi Hendrix in 1968. King was to record an LP, *Live Wire/Blues Power*, at the same venue later that year and was subsequently to become a regular performer there. Albert's distinctive licks were soon being widely imitated by both white and black guitarists. Hendrix, Eric Clapton, Stevie Ray Vaughan, and Robert Cray are among the many top players who have acknowledged their debt to him.

Albert King left Stax in 1974, and none of his subsequent recordings measured up, in terms of sales or quality, to his classic sides for that label. However, he remained immensely popular in concert, despite being forced to reduce his heavy workload in the 1980s due to health problems. He frequently played alongside his namesake B.B. King (the two were not related) up until the early 1990s and had plans for a major European tour prior to his sudden death, from a heart attack, on December 21, 1992.

Albert King's combination of the blues and Memphis soul helped to give him crossover appeal during the late 1960s and 1970s, indirectly broadening the audience for the blues.

B.B. King

b.1925

With the retirement or death of so many of his contemporaries, Riley B. King is now one of the few still-active bluesmen to have been raised on a Mississippi cotton plantation. While growing up, he sang in gospel groups, but also developed a love for the "Devil's music"—to the displeasure of his strictly religious family. He took up guitar in his mid-teens, and after several years of combining farm laboring with singing and busking, he moved to the Memphis area in 1946, and devoted himself full-time to performing.

In Memphis, King built up a following as a blues player and broadcaster, acquiring the nickname Blues Boy (hence his famous initials) in 1949, while working as a DJ on a local radio station, WDIA. Later that year, he made his first records, and in 1952, had a number 1 in the R&B charts with "Three O'Clock Blues." A stream of further hits followed, combined with a tireless schedule of live shows that first brought King stardom on the Southern "chitlin' circuit" and soon established him farther afield. In the 1960s, he was among the first black blues artists to gain a substantial following with white rock audiences, particularly during the latter part of the decade, when he played at rock festivals and opened for The Rolling Stones. He started the 1970s with a U.S. Top 20 single, a cover of Roy Hawkins's "The Thrill Is Gone," and kept the blues torch burning during the rest of the decade—not a good time for the blues in general—with inspiring live performances. Over the following decades, his extensive tours and best-selling albums have made him one of America's most internationally famous musicians. He appeared alongside U2 in their 1988 film *Rattle and Hum*, which introduced him to a new generation of fans; King performed with the band on "When Love Comes To Town." Despite suffering from diabetes, King maintains a rigorous touring schedule of about 300 concerts per year. He is still producing new recordings, too: the year 2000 saw a collaboration with Eric Clapton, *Riding With The King*.

B.B. King cuts a smooth, urbane figure both on- and offstage, but his singing and playing are full of carefully controlled emotion. Unlike some rougher-edged bluesmen, he is a master of dynamics: "Lucille," his Gibson electric guitar, can respond to his touch with a whisper or a full-throated roar. His instrumental work perfectly complements his vocals (King never plays while he is actually singing and is supported by a tightly drilled backing band), and his mostly single-string solos are enhanced by a superb left-hand technique that creates pitch-bends, vibrato, and inflections as subtle as those of any slide guitarist. King's intensity and passion are captured at their peak on the classic LP *Live at the Regal*, made at a Chicago theater in 1964, and regarded by many critics as his finest recording.

Controlled emotion personified. Blues legend B.B. King and "Lucille," photographed during a performance at London's Alexandra Palace in July 1979.

Freddie King

Freddie King made his reputation in the 1960s with a series of deft, concise instrumentals that were perfect for jukeboxes and radio, and were quickly taken up by other performers. Born in Gilmer, Texas, he began playing acoustic guitar as a child, inspired by legendary blues performers such as Big Bill Broonzy, Lightnin' Hopkins, and Blind Lemon Jefferson, but switched to electric after hearing Chicago blues. By the early 1950s, his family had moved to the Windy City, and the young King was listening to his new musical heroes (including Muddy Waters and his sideman Jimmy Rogers) in the flesh, and developing his playing style under their influence.

King joined harmonica player Little Sonny Cooper's band in 1953 and recorded with them for Parrot Records. When the label folded, he switched to El-Bee Records, cutting his first solo record, "Country Boy," in 1956. However, his big break came three years later, when he signed to Federal in Cincinnati, and enjoyed no less than six R&B chart entries with his early singles for the company. Two of the biggest sellers, "Hide Away" and "San-Ho-Zay" (both 1961), were instrumentals; and though King was an accomplished singer, it was solos such as those he performed on these numbers that made his name. Both tracks displayed the vigorous thumb-and-forefinger picking Freddie learned from Jimmy Rogers, in addition to a distinctive range of sounds—ringing treble contrasted with throaty bass on "Hide Away," a funky, overdriven timbre for "San-Ho-Zay"—and an irresistible rhythmic pulse.

Many of King's subsequent sides for Federal were worthy successors to these classics, but he scored no further hits with the label. This lack of chart success had little effect on his popularity, however: like most bluesmen, he relied on live work to make ends meet, and kept up a daunting schedule of one-nighters throughout the decade. Although his success was showing signs of abating Stateside during the mid-1960s, King retained a following in the U.K., in part because of his influence on young white guitarists who were discovering the blues at the time. Peter Green, of John Mayall's Bluesbreakers and Fleetwood Mac, borrowed from King's style, as did fellow ex-Bluesbreaker and one-time Rolling Stone Mick Taylor, and English guitarist Stan Webb, whose group Chicken Shack supported King on his 1967 U.K. tour. King stayed with Federal until 1968, and, after a spell with Atlantic, was signed in 1970 by Shelter, a label run by rock musician (and Freddie King fan) Leon Russell. A little later, Freddie collaborated with another celebrated admirer, Eric Clapton, who had covered "Hide Away" in 1965, and now played on and produced King's LP *Burglar* (1974).

King's association with Clapton brought him wide exposure, but unfortunately he did not live long enough to capitalize on his new success. He died of heart failure, aged only 42, after collapsing at a gig in Dallas on December 29, 1976.

Freddie King's searing solos were a formative influence on U.K. R&B-influenced guitarists of the 1960s, such as Eric Clapton and Peter Green. He is shown here during the 1970s.

Mark Knopfler

b.1949

Mark Knopfler's route to school in the northern English city of Newcastle led past a music store. Knopfler would usually stop to admire the expensive American guitars in the window, and then head for woodwork class to watch avidly as a fellow pupil attempted to build a replica of a Fender electric guitar. It was several years before Knopfler's finances could stretch to one of the instruments he coveted, but his eventual acquisition of a 1961 fiesta red Stratocaster proved to be, quite literally, a passport to success—it was the guitar he used to record "Sultans of Swing" (1978), his first hit with Dire Straits. (The band was named—ironically, in retrospect—for their lean financial circumstances at the time.)

"Sultans of Swing" showcases many of the key characteristics of Knopfler's playing, such as the tight chords and riffs punctuating his laid-back vocals and the sensitive right-hand technique (he invariably uses bare fingers, not picks). He has remained closely associated with the distinctively light yet powerful sound of the Strat since the early days of the group. Significantly, it was the model of guitar favored by one of his musical heroes, Hank Marvin of The Shadows. Knopfler's other major influences include Chuck Berry, B.B. King, and Eric Clapton, though J.J. Cale may also be clearly detected in his soft, bluesy touch and clean picking—as well as in his somewhat gruff singing style. Knopfler's particular love of blues and folk is reflected in his skillful use of acoustic instruments on Dire Straits tracks such as "Romeo And Juliet" (1980), to which his National resonator guitar adds a special poignancy, and the opening of the seven-minute epic "Private Investigations" (1982). The group's enormous mainstream appeal resulted in staggering record sales worldwide (*Brothers In Arms* was one of the biggest-selling albums of the 1980s). However, he retained a certain lyrical bite in his songwriting—"Money For Nothing," featuring an infectiously catchy riff, satirized the then-new channel MTV. The song provided the band with a U.S. number 1 hit.

Due to extended gaps in Dire Straits' touring and recording schedule since the late 1980s (the group's most recent major commitment was their 1991–1992 world tour), Knopfler has had the time to pursue a wide range of alternative musical activities. These have included his film soundtracks for *Local Hero* (1983), *Cal* (1984), and *The Princess Bride* (1987), production credits on albums by Bob Dylan and Randy Newman, and a collaboration with Steve Phillips and Brendan Croker in the band The Notting Hillbillies. Knopfler has also produced an outstanding duo album with country picker Chet Atkins, *Neck And Neck* (1990), containing superb instrumental work from both players on numbers such as the up-tempo "Poor Boy Blues" and the more leisurely "Tahitian Skies." Knopfler has issued two solo CDs, *Golden Heart* (1996), and, most recently, *Sailing to Philadelphia* (2000), which features contributions from Van Morrison, James Taylor, and Chris Difford and Glenn Tilbrook from U.K. band Squeeze.

Dire Straits' success is due in large part to Mark Knopfler's trademark guitar sound. His rapid, clean picking led many to regard him as the finest U.K. blues-derived guitarist since Eric Clapton.

Leo Kottke

b.1945

Leo Kottke became fascinated by the guitar after dabbling with a toy instrument as an 11-year-old boy; he soon acquired a full-size acoustic, and by his teenage years, playing it had become an obsession. His skill and enthusiasm were unaffected by two subsequent mishaps that left him with impaired hearing: one eardrum was damaged by a firecracker, the other by the sound of gunfire during his brief stint in the U.S. Naval Reserve. After dropping out of college in Minnesota, he embarked on a career as a solo guitarist and singer.

Kottke played his first live dates during the mid-1960s, by which time he had developed a fervent interest in the blues and would eagerly check out any local appearances by respected blues artists. By the end of the decade, he had built up a strong local following around his home in Minneapolis, attracting wider attention when his album *Six and Twelve-String Guitar* was released on folk guitarist John Fahey's record label, Takoma, in 1969. Shortly afterward, Kottke landed a deal with a major company, Capitol, and went on to make a string of successful LPs for them and for Chrysalis throughout the 1970s. During this period, he also appeared all over the U.S. and Europe as an opening act for numerous leading rock bands.

His performances gave the lie to anyone inclined to dismiss the acoustic guitar as soft-voiced and musically restricted. Playing with fingerpicks to produce an incisive, driving sound, and making especially resourceful use of the rich sonorities of his 12-string, Kottke created imaginative, quirky arrangements of traditional numbers such as "Cripple Creek" (1971) and "All Through The Night" (1974), and also featured breathtaking original instrumentals, as well as a wide range of songs delivered in his characteristically downbeat vocal style. Kottke's playing drew on a refreshingly broad aural palette, ranging from flurries of notes played at high speed to long, sustained notes from which he sought to extract every nuance of sound.

Unfortunately, during the early 1980s, Kottke began to suffer from tendonitis—a debilitating condition exacerbated by his extensive touring and powerful right-hand technique—which forced him to cut back on live performances and adapt his playing style. Abandoning his fingerpicks in favor of an approach more usually associated with classical guitarists, he unveiled a new, less percussive sound on the reflective *A Shout Towards Noon* (1986), which revealed an even greater sensitivity to tone than he had previously displayed. More recently, Kottke has experimented with jazzier harmonies, relied less on the open tunings he used in his earlier work, and developed his songwriting and singing. However, he still retains some old favorites in his repertoire, and is considered as influential and highly respected as ever by acoustic guitar devotees.

A gifted player of both six-string and 12-string acoustic guitar, Leo Kottke has embraced blues, folk, bluegrass, country, rock, and jazz. He is shown here during the mid-1980s.

Eddie Lang

1902–1933

Eddie Lang is widely acknowledged as the first significant jazz guitarist. His pioneering solo and accompaniment work paved the way for two titans of the instrument—Charlie Christian and Django Reinhardt—and enabled the guitar to supersede the banjo as a vital element of jazz combos and dance bands in the 1930s. He was also a major influence on players such as Tal Farlow and George Van Eps, who came to prominence during the 1950s. In short, without Eddie Lang, there is little doubt that the evolution of jazz guitar music would have been very different.

Born Salvatore Massaro in Philadelphia on October 25, 1902, Eddie was the son of a guitar maker; he took his new name from a basketball hero. He started learning the violin from an early age but switched to the guitar by the time he was 10 years old. He went to the same high school as Joe Venuti, a gifted violin player, and they became friends and musical allies up until the guitarist's premature death; their early recordings anticipated the Django Reinhardt and Stephane Grappelli Hot Club recordings of the mid-1930s.

After working with bands in his home town, Lang joined the Mound City Blue Blowers in 1924. They had a hit with "Arkansas Blue" and subsequently toured Europe and the U.K. A year later, with the reputation of being America's best jazz guitarist, Lang left the band to work with some of the top musicians of the day. His single note solos with Bix Beiderbecke and the Dorsey Brothers marked the beginning of the guitar as a lead instrument in jazz. Lang specialized in dazzling one-string solos, something that was later to become a feature of many jazz and blues guitarists, including Reinhardt. Composers and arrangers heard Lang and began to include guitar solo parts in their arrangements.

Lang did not restrict himself exclusively to the jazz field, however. In the 1920s he recorded some blues numbers under the alias Blind Willie Dunn, and in 1928, under his own name, recorded a version of Rachmaninoff's "Prelude" for guitar. From 1928 to 1929, under the Dunn pseudonym, he recorded a set of acclaimed guitar duets with blues guitarist Lonnie Johnson (another single-string solo specialist), on which the two selflessly alternated rhythm and lead parts to memorable effect. The same year, Lang was hired to play in Paul Whiteman's orchestra. He became friends with one of Whiteman's singers, Bing Crosby, and became the crooner's full-time accompanist. Crosby even persuaded Lang to appear in two of his films: *The King of Jazz* (1930) and *The Big Broadcast* (1932).

By the early 1930s, Lang had become the most sought-after jazz guitarist in the world and one of the best-paid musicians of the day. Tragically, he died at the peak of his career, on March 26, 1933, after complications set in following a routine tonsillectomy operation. The jazz world had abruptly lost one of its great pioneers.

Eddie Lang's brief but dynamic career saw him transform the guitar into a lead instrument in jazz, paving the way for later guitar greats such as Charlie Christian and Django Reinhardt.

Paco de Lucía

b.1947

Paco de Lucía is generally regarded as the leading flamenco guitarist of his generation. However, while remaining true to the spirit of this music, he has also worked extensively with performers from different cultural backgrounds, and has won wide acclaim for his innovative stylistic fusions.

Paco was born Francisco Sánchez Gómez in the southern Spanish port of Algeciras. His first guitar teacher was his father, Antonio, and Paco made his musical debut on a local radio station at the age of 11. He made his first recording in 1961, *Los Chiquitos De Algeciras*, on which he accompanied his brother Pepe. As a teenager, he adopted the stage name de Lucía, and joined dancer José Greco's flamenco troupe, visiting New York with them in 1963. He continued to tour extensively over the following years, eventually releasing his first solo album, *La Fabulosa Guittara De Paco De Lucía*, in 1967. This record, a collection of pieces in standard flamenco forms, already revealed a breathtaking virtuosity. On numbers such as "En la Caleta," Paco's high-velocity runs and elaborate right-hand decorations seemed to burst out of his instrument—like most flamenco players, he uses a bright-toned, cypress-bodied guitar—with a raw, fiery immediacy. However, on later LPs he began to develop a distinctively radical approach to the genre, a "new" flamenco that fused outside elements with the traditional flamenco form. A trip to Brazil had fired Lucía with enthusiasm for South American instruments and rhythms. This manifested itself on *Fuente Y Candal* (1973), which included a rumba, "Entre Dos Aguas," played with bass guitar and Latin-American percussion backing. The track went on to become a hit single in Spain, and Paco's subsequent album, *Almoraima* (1976), also featured bass and other nontraditional elements.

Paco's passion for musical experimentation subsequently led to a long and fruitful association with jazz fusion guitarist John McLaughlin. One of the highlights of their musical partnership was the live album *Friday Night In San Francisco* (1981), which captures a concert of extraordinary excitement and intensity given by de Lucía, McLaughlin, and fellow guitarist Al Di Meola at San Francisco's Warfield Theater in December 1980. The trio have performed and recorded together on several later occasions, and de Lucía has gone on to work with pianist Chick Corea and other notable jazz artists.

Paco's most recent projects have been diverse in nature, ranging from film and ballet scores to a guest appearance on a single by rock star Bryan Adams. However, he remains deeply committed to his musical roots, and received lavish praise for his 1998 CD *Luzia* (1998), recorded with a small group and described by one critic as "a profound portrait of the soul of flamenco."

"You grab tradition with one hand, and with the other you scratch, you search." Guitarist Paco de Lucía has given flamenco a new lease of life by incorporating elements from other cultures.

Franco L. Makiadi

1938–1989

François Luambo Makiadi was born in a village in the Belgian Congo (now Zaire). As a child, he moved with his mother to the capital city of Léopoldville (later Kinchasa), where he began playing guitar at the age of seven. His first instrument was homemade—a guitar made out of tin cans that featured stripped electrical wire for strings. Four years later, he was appearing with a local band, Watama, and soon afterward, he started working as a studio musician. By this time he had started to develop a definite style of his own, creating a hard, urgent sound that featured some smart fingerpicking. Coupled with his boyish good looks, his prodigious musical talents soon made him a popular recording star.

In 1956, Franco (as he was now known), cofounded OK Jazz, a group named for the OK Bar in Léopoldville. The lineup comprised vocals, saxophone, bass, and percussion as well as two guitarists, and the group's style fused Latin-American rumba rhythms with a distinctive Congolese feel. On some of their early recordings, Franco played acoustic guitar, but he switched to electric as OK Jazz began to expand and develop, and his melodious, reverberant solo lines and riffs became one of the band's trademarks. Often based around sweet-sounding intervals such as sixths or tenths, his guitar sometimes took center stage, but often shared the limelight with other instruments—as on "Finga Mama Munu" (1966)—or elegantly complemented the band's vocalists and rhythm section.

By the mid-1960s, OK Jazz had added "TP" (standing for "Tout Puissant") to their name, and were the most popular musicians in their newly independent country. Franco had begun to introduce vocal, rhythmic, and guitar elements from Congolese folklore into the group's music by this time, and was regarded as the leader. He was becoming famous not only as a guitarist and singer, but also for the social commentary and satire contained in his lyrics. In particular, he began to make observations on (and criticisms of) the moves toward modernization that he saw in his society. Many of his songs about Zairean life were benign—"Azda" (1973) was a paean of praise to a Kinchasa automobile dealer—but after releasing the sexually explicit "Jackie" a year later, he found himself (briefly) in jail. In 1980 he recorded "Tailleur," a dance number subtly lampooning the Zairean prime minister.

However, such barbs did not affect Franco's status as Zaire's most eminent performer. He continued to lead TPOK Jazz throughout the 1980s, but following the band's 30th anniversary celebrations in 1986, rumors about his health began to circulate. In 1987 he issued the poignant and powerful "Attention La SIDA" ("Beware of AIDS"), but succumbed to the disease himself two years later.

Known in his native Zaire as "The Sorcerer of the Guitar," Franco Luambo Makiadi produced a driving, metallic sound from his instrument. During his career, Makiadi wrote hundreds of songs, providing a commentary on the monumental changes affecting his country.

Joe Maphis

1921–1986

Joe Maphis was a pioneer of country guitar picking and expanded the instrument's dynamic range dramatically during the 1950s. Today, he is recognized as one of the first musicians to use the guitar as a lead instrument in country music, a genre in which the fiddle had hitherto dominated solo work. His formidable picking took guitar techniques to a higher level, helping to pave the way for later, "fast" country-rock players such as Albert Lee, Steve Morse, and Ricky Skaggs.

Otis W. ("Joe") Maphis was born in Suffolk, Virginia on May 12, 1921. His father taught him to play the fiddle at an early age and he was soon performing at country dances; by the time he was a teenager, Maphis was competent on the guitar, banjo, and just about every other stringed instrument. As a 16-year-old, he was a regular on radio station WBRA Richmond, by which time he was also proving himself a more than capable bass player. He appeared with the Lazy K Ranch Boys and also starred in several top country radio shows during the late 1930s and 1940s, including *Boone County Jamboree*, *National Barn Dance*, and *Old Dominion Barn Dance*.

Maphis met a well-known country singer, Rose Lee (a.k.a. Rose of the Mountains) in 1948. They married in 1952 and became a successful husband-and-wife duo, regularly appearing on radio broadcast shows such as *Hometown Jamboree* and *Town Hall Party* (later televised) during the early 1950s. They also recorded a series of albums including *King of the Strings* (1962), *Rose Lee And Joe Maphis* (1962), *Mr. And Mrs. Country Music* (1964), and *Gospel Guitar* (1968). One of their songs, "Dim Lights, Thick Smoke, and Loud, Loud Music" became a country standard. Joe and Rose Lee performed as a duo until 1985, appearing on the popular TV program *Hee-Haw* during those final years.

Although Joe was seen as a country artist in his own right, he was also known for his excellent instrumental session work with artists such as Ricky Nelson, Tex Ritter, and Wanda Jackson. In 1954 he acquired a double-necked guitar, using it to record the song for which he is perhaps best known—"Fire On The Strings," an adaptation of the traditional tune "Fire On The Mountain," originally arranged for fiddle. In the 1950s, Maphis's multi-instrumental skills, especially his work on the famous twin-necked instrument, made him an in-demand musician and saw him perform on the soundtracks for a number of films, including *God's Little Acre* (1958). During the following decade, he featured on the incidental music for many well-known TV programs, including *The Virginian* and *FBI Story*, and also collaborated with guitar legend Merle Travis on two groundbreaking country guitar recordings—*Merle Travis And Joe Maphis* (1964) and *Country Guitar Giants* (1979). Maphis died of lung cancer in Nashville on June 27, 1986.

Nicknamed "The King of the Strings" for his extraordinarily rapid picking, Maphis ranks with Chet Atkins and Merle Travis among the finest country guitarists of all time.

Johnny Marr

b.1963

Growing up in the city of Manchester during the late 1970s, budding guitarist John Maher was unimpressed by the punk rock then dominating the pop scene. His tastes drew on a broader range of influences than many of his peers, often harking back to an earlier era: he loved the sound of classic Motown groups such as The Temptations and The Marvelettes, and among his favorite guitarists were folk-inspired British players such as John Martyn, Richard Thompson, and Bert Jansch. These eclectic influences fed Maher's refreshing musical originality, and by the early 1980s he had become a key figure in contemporary Manchester rock circles. In 1982, he met singer and lyricist Stephen Patrick Morrissey, forming a songwriting partnership that led to the creation of The Smiths. At around this time, he renamed himself Marr to avoid confusion with John Maher, drummer with Mancunian punk legends the Buzzcocks.

Between 1983 and 1987, The Smiths had a string of British hit singles—all of which were dominated by Morrissey's dark wit and Marr's layered, tuneful guitars—and released five best-selling albums. Marr's work with the group reflected his admiration for The Byrds and The Beatles, but also contained an aural kaleidoscope of other colors and allusions. There are touches of crunchy glam rock guitar in songs such as "Sheila Take A Bow" (1987), and even a hint of West African highlife in his jingle-jangle picking on "This Charming Man" (1983) and "Ask" (1986). Marr's rich instrumental textures (he rarely takes lengthy solos) provided a perfect setting for Morrissey's vocals, and sometimes, as on "Girlfriend In A Coma" (1987), formed a wonderfully ironic contrast to the subject matter of the numbers the two wrote together.

After the break-up of The Smiths in 1987, Marr, who had already collaborated on Bryan Ferry's album *Bête Noire* (1987), soon found himself in demand from other major names. He went on to guest with Talking Heads and The Pretenders, recorded and toured as a member of cult English band The The, and enjoyed substantial chart success with Electronic (also featuring fellow Manchester musician Bernard Sumner from New Order) throughout the 1990s. In recent years, Marr's projects have included an appearance on Bert Jansch's *Crimson Moon* CD (2000), as well as concerts and sessions with his own band, The Healers, although it is his brilliant work with The Smiths for which he is most fondly remembered. His knowledge of diverse musical forms and sheer technical ability have meant that Marr's guitar playing has had few direct imitators, although he is undoubtedly one of the key figures in the history of English popular music. "When The Smiths came on *Top Of The Tops* for the first time, that was it for me," Noel Gallagher of Oasis once revealed. "From that day on I wanted to be Johnny Marr."

The finest English rock guitarist of his generation. Johnny Marr in 1987, after four years of playing with one of the U.K.'s most defiantly original groups, The Smiths.

Hank Marvin

b.1941

At the end of the 1950s, a time when British pop music was a pale imitation of its American counterpart, singer Cliff Richard and his backing band The Drifters (soon to be renamed The Shadows to avoid confusion with the American vocal group of the same name) were the only U.K. act that came close to generating the excitement associated with Elvis Presley or Buddy Holly. Their music, like Cliff's Presley-derived onstage gyrations, was directly inspired by U.S. models. The group's lead guitarist, Hank Marvin, had taught himself to play by copying Scotty Moore and James Burton licks from records and the radio. Following his group's first chart success, he became one of the first Britons to acquire a Fender Stratocaster (then almost impossible to obtain in the U.K. due to import restrictions); and the twangy sound he coaxed from it with the aid of a tape echo unit owed a clear debt to Duane Eddy.

However, Marvin and the other Shadows used these American influences to create a classic (and distinctively British-sounding) series of instrumentals during the 1960s, while simultaneously continuing their successful association with Cliff Richard. Their hits, including "Apache" (1960)—which, ironically, knocked Cliff's own "Please Don't Tease" from the U.K. number 1 spot—"Kon-Tiki" (1961), and "Wonderful Land" (1962), were all dominated by Hank's crisp, melodious guitar work, which also utilized tremolo. So successful was The Shadows' musical formula that they became the dominant group in the U.K. between the decline of skiffle at the end of the 1950s and the rise of The Beatles and Merseybeat in 1963.

The relative simplicity and accessibility of Hank's style undoubtedly encouraged budding guitarists of the day. They flocked in their thousands to the band's concerts to study his playing, and many of today's biggest U.K. rock names have acknowledged the inspiration that The Shadows gave them. Among them is Mark Knopfler, who, in 1985, realized his lifelong ambition to perform "Wonderful Land" on stage with Hank.

The Shadows had employed strings on "Wonderful Land," softening their sound, and future hits became gradually more mainstream in nature. However, the hits began to dry up as the decade wore on and The Shadows began to appear increasingly out of touch with contemporary trends. The band finally broke up in 1968, but re-formed in the 1970s, achieving two Top 10 U.K. hits with "Don't Cry For Me Argentina" and "Theme From The Deer Hunter (Cavatina)." Marvin is now based in Australia but continues to record with the latest version of the group and to issue regular solo albums, although much of his output is now "middle-of-the-road" or nostalgic in flavor. In 1996, the group's glory days were celebrated by the release of *Twang!—A Tribute To Hank Marvin And The Shadows*, an album featuring reworkings of their greatest hits by a distinguished cast of players including Peter Green, Mark Knopfler, Brian May, and Marvin himself.

The U.K.'s first guitar hero. Hank Marvin's clean, economical playing style has influenced generations of guitarists. He is shown here with his Fender Stratocaster onstage in 1977.

Brian May

b.1947

The young Brian May was academically gifted, obsessed with music, and, by his teenage years, sufficiently adept at woodworking and practical electronics to build his own electric guitar—named the "Red Special"—with a little assistance from his father. They constructed the instrument using wood from a nineteenth-century fireplace, incorporating movable pickups that allowed May to produce a wide range of tones.

The Red Special has remained May's instrument of choice ever since: he first used it onstage with one of his first groups, 1984, in the early 1960s. Later, it accompanied him to London University, where he studied physics and astronomy. At college, he and a fellow student, drummer Roger Taylor, started a new band, Smile; the group made a U.S.-only single in 1969, but broke up the following year. May and Taylor then formed Queen with a mutual friend, singer Freddie Mercury; bassist John Deacon joined them in 1971. After an extensive period of rehearsal and recording, the group released their first album, *Queen* (1973). Each member of Queen was a capable songwriter—all four were to pen Top 10 hits during the band's career—although the partnership of Mercury and May produced most of the material.

Queen's early demos were engineered by Roy Thomas Baker, who went on to produce many of their biggest hits. Baker's technical ingenuity was crucial to the development of Brian May's distinctive sound. On "Killer Queen" (1974), and on several subsequent songs, his skillful multitracking intertwines May's instrumental harmonies so perfectly with Freddie Mercury's similarly layered vocals that it is sometimes difficult to distinguish voices from guitars. The slightly hollow resonance of the Red Special's pickups adds to the rich sonic blend, as does May's precise control over attack and vibrato (he uses ultra-light gauge strings and picks with a small coin).

Other Queen classics, from "Bohemian Rhapsody" (1975) onward, feature set-piece solos in which May's guitar histrionics are devastatingly effective. His work never displays the blues-derived clichés that were the staple of so many other stadium rockers of the 1970s and 1980s, but reflects and enhances the band's unique combination of theatricality, raunchiness, and kitsch—and provides an ideal musical foil for Freddie Mercury's singing and keyboards.

Despite Queen's phenomenal worldwide success, Brian May has continued to pursue his own creative avenues. In 1989, he collaborated with other rock stars, including Robert Plant and Iron Maiden's Bruce Dickinson, on a remake of the Deep Purple classic "Smoke On The Water" to raise funds for the victims of an earthquake in Armenia. The following year saw him compose the score for a London production of *Macbeth*. Since Mercury's death in 1991, May has had a highly successful solo career, releasing two studio albums—*Back To The Light* (1992) and *Another World* (1998)—as well as a live CD recorded at London's Brixton Academy.

Using a self-made instrument, Brian May has become one of rock's most distinctive guitarists. His flamboyant appearance in this photo typifies Queen's over-the-top 1970s stage gear.

John McLaughlin

b.1942

John McLaughlin was the first guitarist to bridge the gap between jazz and rock. His guitar playing on Miles Davis's seminal fusion albums during the early 1970s mixed jazz licks and rock power in a way that hadn't been heard before. He was also the founding member of a pioneering jazz-rock group that inspired both rock and jazz musicians for more than three decades.

John was born near Doncaster, England, on January 4, 1942. His mother and three brothers were also musicians and he started taking piano lessons at the age of nine; however, after hearing recordings by blues guitarists Muddy Waters and Leadbelly, he switched over to the guitar. By the time he was 15 he was listening to Django Reinhardt and Tal Farlow, and leading his own jazz band at school. He broadened his influences further by listening to cool jazz by Miles Davis and orchestral music by composers such as Bartok and Stravinsky. He moved to London when he was 21 and got his first major musical job as guitarist with the Graham Bond Organisation. Subsequently he worked with Bond, Georgie Fame, and Brian Auger, all of whom played R&B with jazz overtones, and rapidly became known for his virtuosity, particularly his ability to play lengthy phrases at high speed.

McLaughlin left England in 1969 and arrived in the U.S. to work with jazz drummer Tony Williams, who had won widespread admiration for his work with Miles Davis. Williams's band, Lifetime, featured both McLaughlin and bassist Jack Bruce, who had previously worked together in the Graham Bond Organisation. Davis heard John's playing with Lifetime and subsequently asked him to participate in the recordings that were to fuse jazz and rock for the first time—*In A Silent Way* (1969) and *Bitches Brew* (1970). McLaughlin's funky, staccato riffs played a crucial role on these albums.

Inspired by Eastern mysticism, McLaughlin left Miles in 1971 to form his own group, the Mahavishnu Orchestra. Their explosive creativity broke new boundaries in jazz in terms of virtuosity and complexity, stunning audiences worldwide. The album, *The Inner Mounting Flame* (1971), which combined raga rhythms and themes with electric guitar, is regarded today as a fusion classic. Four years later, McLaughlin turned away from electric music and formed Shakti, a celebrated acoustic band that drew on Eastern influences and featured top Indian musicians including L. Shankar (violin) and Zakir Hussain (tablas). During this period, McLaughlin experimented with sitarlike drones, using a customized guitar with raised frets. He later formed an acoustic guitar trio with another fusion ace, Al Di Meola, and flamenco virtuoso Paco de Lucía for the breathtaking *Friday Night In San Francisco* (1981). His music remains both progressive and stimulating.

John McLaughlin, seen here during the late 1980s, was one of the leading lights of fusion. His subsequent work has seen the guitarist embrace Eastern spirituality and other world influences.

Blind Willie McTell

1901–1959

Blind Willie McTell is best known for his "Statesboro Blues," named for the town in Georgia where he grew up; the song was covered in the mid-1960s by Taj Mahal, and later by The Allman Brothers Band. Despite an extensive recording career (boosted by the use of pseudonyms, which enabled him to appear on several different labels), none of McTell's own disks ever sold especially well, and his distinctive singing and playing style have not been widely emulated. Nevertheless, he is now recognized as a unique figure in blues history, and is renowned for his mastery of an instrument frequently consigned by lesser musicians to simple rhythm work—the 12-string guitar.

Blind from birth, McTell learned the basics of music from his mother, developing his technique during his teens and twenties, while appearing in carnivals and traveling shows. His records (the first of which were made in Atlanta for the Victor company in 1927) capture his subtle approach to the blues. McTell's high, clear vocals are set against the rich sonorities of his Stella 12-string, often tuned to a low pitch and sometimes played with a bottleneck. He makes light of the difficulties of picking the guitar's double courses with bare fingers, and on songs such as "Savannah Mama" (1933), creates an almost pianolike texture with his combination of deep bass, slide lines, and chords. Other numbers combine intricacy and excitement—especially "Georgia Rag" (1931), which gathers speed and complexity as Willie exhorts himself to "Swing that Georgia Rag, boy!"

Although it is for his 12-string work that McTell is most renowned, he was also proficient on a six-string acoustic, accordion, kazoo, violin, and harmonica. McTell's vocals further distinguished him from many contemporary blues performers: high, understated, and sensitively delivered, his singing has been compared to that of a white vocalist performing in a black vocal style.

McTell's musical career took him all over the U.S. and he worked up a broad range of songs including rags, ballads, popular tunes, and folk standards, as well as blues numbers. He once commented that "I was born a rambler [and] I'm gonna ramble until I die," and his versatility and wide repertoire meant that he was able to perform (in the words of blues expert David Evans) "virtually anywhere a crowd might be gathered." However, in later years, he spent most of his time working near his Atlanta home. Folk archivist John Lomax came across McTell singing on an Atlanta street corner in 1940 and went on to record him playing a series of blues ballads, gospel numbers, and spoken narratives about his life for the Library of Congress. In his later years, McTell increasingly abandoned the blues in favor of gospel songs. He died, following a stroke, in a hospital at Milledgeville, southeast of Atlanta, on August 19, 1959.

A unique figure in blues history, Blind Willie McTell has no obvious musical ancestors or descendants; his distinctive vocals and skilled 12-string playing made him a true original.

Pat Metheny

b.1954

Pat Metheny is perhaps the most popular jazz guitarist in the world today. His records enjoy excellent sales compared to other jazz releases and his concerts regularly sell out around the world. He is also considered by many of his peers to be one of the most inspired and influential jazz composers in the history of the genre.

Metheny was born in Lee's Summit, Missouri, on August 12, 1954. His first instrument was the French horn, but he took up the guitar as a teenager. Metheny studied music at the University of Miami and his precocious virtuosity led to guitar teaching posts—both in Miami and at the Berklee College of Music in Boston—while he was still in his teens. His first professional break came in 1974 when he became a member of vibraphonist Gary Burton's quintet. The group produced three albums, on each of which Metheny's smooth guitar playing, reminiscent of Wes Montgomery, played a prime role.

When Manfred Eicher, producer with ECM Records, heard the young guitarist, he was impressed enough to offer him a recording contract. Teaming up with Lyle Mays (keyboards), Mark Egan (bass), and Danny Gottlieb (drums), Metheny formed the Pat Metheny Group in 1977. Their eponymously named debut album forged a new, earthy and mellow jazz sound, incorporating elements from bebop, folk, Latin, rock, and classical music; it took the jazz world by storm.

Later Metheny Group albums, such as *Offramp* (1981), *First Circle* (1984), *Still Life Talking* (1987), and *Secret Story* (1992), reinforced the guitarist's reputation as a gifted composer and performer; many of these albums have gone on to win Grammys. In 1985, Metheny changed direction again, working with David Bowie on the music for John Schlesinger's *The Falcon And The Snowman*. The single "This Is Not America," taken from the film's soundtrack, became a Top 40 hit on both sides of the Atlantic, helping to bring the guitarist to the attention of a more mainstream rock and pop audience.

Metheny has never been one to shy away from music technology and his fascination with electronics led to the inclusion of a Synclavier guitar synthesizer on a number of his recordings. One of his favorite sounds, a soaring trumpetlike tone, can be heard on tracks such as "Are You Going With Me?" (from *Offramp*) and "The Truth Will Always Be" (from *Secret Story*). However, Metheny's appetite for musical boundary stretching has nearly always been tempered by a strong melodic sensibility, which has served him both as a healthy check to self-indulgence and as a means of making his music more accessible, resulting in several hits on the pop album charts. Having also played and recorded with a range of artists, including Joni Mitchell, Ornette Coleman, and John Scofield, Metheny has gained a reputation for being one of the busiest jazz musicians in the world.

Few guitarists have demonstrated such eclecticism as Pat Metheny, whose output has embraced jazz, rock, classical, Latin, and rock, among other genres. He is shown here in 1990.

Wes Montgomery

1923–1968

Wes Montgomery was one of the most influential jazz guitarists ever to have lived. His cool, laid-back style introduced the genre of jazz to a wider audience, and his unusual technique of using his thumb as a pick—developed because he didn't want to disturb the neighbors when practicing—resulted in a a quiet but distinctive style that subsequently influenced other guitar greats as diverse as Joe Pass and Pat Metheny. He was also one of the first solo guitar players to effortlessly mix single notes with octaves and chords.

John Leslie ("Wes") Montgomery was born in Indianapolis on March 6, 1923. He started playing guitar at the relatively late age of 19, but within six months, he was able to play all of Charlie Christian's solos note for note. Montgomery adapted Christian's original playing to suit his own capabilities but also developed stylistic characteristics of his own, such as solos played in octaves and a driving, rhythmic swing. Initially, he played alongside his brothers Monk (bass) and Buddy (vibraphone) in local clubs, to considerable acclaim, but in 1948 he left his hometown to join Lionel Hampton's band, with whom he toured and recorded for two years. However, Montgomery returned to Indianapolis in the early 1950s to play jazz with his brothers, first as the Mastersounds and then as the Montgomery Brothers. The group became an established act in the Indianapolis jazz scene during the latter part of the decade.

The Montgomery Brothers led busy lives, working at their factory jobs by day and playing at a local jazz haunt, the Missile Room, by night. Wes's big break came when the renowned saxophonist Julian "Cannonball" Adderley spotted him playing at the Missile Room one evening. Adderley was so impressed by the young guitarist that he called his contacts at the well-known Riverside record company the next day and convinced them to sign Montgomery up. The result was one of the most celebrated jazz guitar recordings of all time: *The Incredible Jazz Guitar Of Wes Montgomery* (1960). Wes went on to become the most popular and influential jazz guitarist of the 1960s, with sell-out performances and critically acclaimed albums including *So Much Guitar* (1961), *Movin' Wes* (1964), and *Smokin' at the Half Note* (1965), described later by Pat Metheny as "the absolute greatest jazz-guitar album ever made." Montgomery's later recordings, such as *Tequila* (1966) and *A Day In The Life* (1967), were of a more accessible nature, the latter proving to be his biggest commercial success. These albums sold well although, perhaps unsurprisingly, they were shunned by jazz purists for their mainstream leanings.

Just when Wes was at the peak of his playing and music career, tragedy struck: he died suddenly of a heart attack on June 15, 1968. Like his earliest influence, Charlie Christian, Wes Montgomery was another jazz guitar genius who led far too short a life.

A quiet storm. Wes Montgomery's understated playing style and lack of showmanship was a reflection of his own warm, undemonstrative nature. He is seen here in the early 1960s.

Ramon Montoya

1880–1949

The roots of flamenco date back as far as 1840. The earliest guitarists who played in this style did not perform solos and were simply required to accompany singers and dancers; most of these musicians had relatively unrefined techniques. However, good guitarists were always in demand and such players would often introduce new tricks into their repertoire in an effort to outdo their peers. This healthy competitiveness resulted in the emergence of a series of great guitar players during the remaining years of the nineteenth century, culminating in Ramon Montoya, the man who, more than any other player, was responsible for turning flamenco guitar into a solo medium.

Ramon was born in Madrid on November 2, 1880. His parents were gypsy cattle traders, and he spent the earliest years of his life working at their side. However, one day, as an adolescent, he chose to spend his earnings on a guitar, a decision that was to change the direction of his life completely. Infatuated with the instrument, Ramon practiced his guitar playing endlessly, incorporating elements of classical guitar into his style—including a variety of arpeggios. He proved so proficient as a guitar player that by the time he reached 14 he was accompanying *cantantes* (singers) in Madrid. Ramon's virtuosity grew rapidly and, during the early twentieth century, he formed a musical allegiance with one of the greatest Spanish singers of the time, Antonio Chacon. The two initially achieved a new level of understanding as singer and player, but Ramon's flamboyant dexterity often became too much for the singer and their relationship gradually deteriorated, with both musicians reputedly hitting each other during their later public performances. They eventually parted company and Ramon continued to overcome other singers with his spectacular playing until, eventually, some adapted the way they sang in order to fit in with what he was playing. This was the start of a process by which the guitar would come to stand as a solo instrument in its own right rather than as an accompaniment; the modern flamenco style was born.

Ramon was the first truly famous flamenco player. He was considerably more popular than those flamenco guitarists who preceded him and, between 1910 and 1940, made more than 700 recordings with top *cantantes*. He was a huge influence on the next generation of flamenco guitarists, including his nephew, Carlos Montoya, who further established the style as a serious form of guitar music between the 1930s and the 1960s. These, in turn, influenced the still-unsurpassed flamenco talents of Paco Peña, Paco de Lucia, Tomatito, Vicente Amigo, Gerardo Nuñez, Juan Mañuel Canizares, and multicultural virtuoso Jorge Strunz.

The father of modern flamenco. Ramon Montoya's brilliance as a musician frequently overshadowed the vocal efforts of the flamenco singers whom he accompanied. On several occasions, enraged by his domination of their set, singers left Montoya alone on the stage.

Scotty Moore

b.1931

Born in Gadsden, Tennessee, Scotty Moore began playing the guitar as a child, and formed his first group in the late 1940s, while serving in the U.S. Navy. Upon returning to civilian life, he moved to Memphis and co-founded the Starlite Wranglers, a country band that recorded a single for Sun Records in spring 1954. Soon afterward, Sun's owner, Sam Phillips, asked Moore and Wranglers bassist Bill Black to back a promising young singer, Elvis Presley, for what was intended as a studio audition. During this session, on July 5, 1954, the trio cut their first classic—a version of Arthur Crudup's "That's All Right,"

Above: The King and his right-hand man. Scotty backs Elvis on a 1950s TV show.

driven by Black's slapped bass and the rounded yet urgent sound of Scotty's Gibson semi-acoustic. On its release, the song only gave Presley a local hit, but marked the start of a musical partnership with Moore, Black (and, later, drummer D.J. Fontana) that would produce some of the greatest rock and roll of all time.

In their early days together, Elvis and his musicians were usually promoted as a group, with Moore acting as manager. He was initially displaced from this position by Bob Neal, whose successor, Colonel Tom Parker, eventually relegated him to the role of hired sideman. Nevertheless, Moore's essential musical importance to Presley remained undiminished, as his memorable guitar work on classics such as "Heartbreak Hotel," "Hound Dog" (both 1956), and "Jailhouse Rock" (1957) shows. However, Elvis's two-year absence on army service between 1958 and 1960 led to Moore becoming increasingly involved in production and sound engineering. Although he continued to play for Presley during the 1960s, he gradually reduced his session-playing commitments after launching his own Nashville studio, Music City Recorders, in 1964. The two men shared a stage for the last time on Elvis's TV comeback special four years later.

Scotty's subsequent appearances as a guitarist have been restricted to occasional reunion concerts and tribute albums, including *All The King's Men* (1997), which featured D.J. Fontana and Keith Richards and Ronnie Wood of The Rolling Stones. In 2000, Moore was inducted into the Rock and Roll Hall of Fame.

Left: Scotty Moore's idiosyncratic guitar sound was a vital element in Elvis's early hits. Here, Presley plays rhythm to Scotty's lead solo in one of their earliest appearances together.

Jimmy Page

b.1944

In the mid-1960s, former art student Jimmy Page was a respected but relatively obscure London session guitarist, whose work featured on releases by The Who and The Kinks, among other musical luminaries. Although his work on mainstream pop records was lucrative, Page found it creatively unfulfilling, and in 1966 he eagerly accepted an invitation to join The Yardbirds, one of Britain's most musically adventurous bands. He stayed with them until their split in the summer of 1968, touring Scandinavia shortly afterward with the "New Yardbirds" (none of them part of the original group) to fulfill outstanding commitments. The other members of the quartet were bassist John Paul Jones, drummer John Bonham, and singer Robert Plant. In October 1968, the foursome made their U.K. debut as Led Zeppelin. The name was inspired by a comment from The Who's Keith Moon, who had quipped that the band would go down like a lead zeppelin.

The year 1969 saw the start of Zeppelin's astonishingly rapid rise to fame; they were soon headlining at major venues on both sides of the Atlantic, and had attained rock superstardom by the early 1970s. At the heart of their unique sound lay Page's eclectic guitar style, with its influences drawn from blues, R&B, English folk, and beyond. In the studio, he demonstrated an acute ear for light and shade, combining acoustic and electric textures on slow-building songs such as "Babe I'm Gonna Leave You" (1969) and "Stairway To Heaven" (1971). "The Battle Of Evermore" (1971) highlighted Page's interest in folk music, mixing mandolins and harmony vocals from Fairport Convention's Sandy Denny to magical effect. Page often "orchestrated" his playing with layers of overdubs, creating drones and other effects by using a violin bow on the guitar strings, a technique pioneered by Eddie Phillips of the British band The Creation. At Zeppelin's gargantuan live shows, there was sometimes less scope for such subtlety, but never any shortage of excitement from Page's high-octane soloing, which set the standard for all future hard rock and heavy metal axemen.

Led Zeppelin's massively successful career (punctuated by stories of wild behavior that remain virtually unsurpassed in rock history) ended in 1980, after the drink-related death of John Bonham. The three surviving band members have since made occasional appearances together, joined by Bonham's son Jason on drums, but much of Page's best recent work has been achieved in partnership with Robert Plant, including notable collaborations on the albums *No Quarter—Unledded* (1994) and *Walking Into Clarksdale* (1998). The former augmented Page's guitar playing with Celtic and Arabic rhythms, also featuring a string section and a 16-piece Egyptian orchestra. Such an appetite for innovation, combined with the commercial success of both albums, suggests that Jimmy Page's days as a music legend are far from over.

In full flight, onstage with Led Zeppelin in the mid-1970s. Page's twin-necked Gibson guitar helped him re-create the range of guitar sounds heard on tracks such as "Stairway To Heaven."

Joe Pass

Joe Pass was one of the most popular jazz guitar players to emerge during the 1960s. Using a phenomenal right-handed finger technique, he was able to play melodies, chords, and bass lines, all at the same time. He often performed as a solo artist, demonstrating this dexterity to astounded jazz audiences all over the world, but he was also an excellent single-string improviser, as many of his recordings for the Pablo label testify.

Pass was born Joseph Anthony Passalaqua in New Brunswick, New Jersey, on January 13, 1929. He started playing the guitar at the age of nine, and within a couple of years was regularly putting in eight hours' practice every day. By the time he was 15, Pass was playing regularly in local dance bands. He fell in love with jazz as soon as he heard it and rapidly set about learning Charlie Parker solos note for note. Pass progressed quickly and was playing with Tony Astor's band before he had even left high school. Charlie Christian's startling innovations certainly registered with the young Pass, although his chief guitar influences were to be Django Reinhardt, Wes Montgomery, and Tal Farlow. However, jazz horn players made an even greater impression on him, particularly with regard to phrasing, and he listened long and hard to the work of Parker, Stan Getz, Dizzy Gillespie, and Coleman Hawkins. The study paid off—before long, Pass was performing innovative bebop solos of extraordinary speed, earning himself the nickname "president of bebop guitar."

In 1949, Pass moved to New York in an attempt to mingle with some of the finest exponents of the genre. Unfortunately, he spent more time associating with dope dealers and he soon developed a drug habit, for which he had to serve time. In 1961 he entered the Synanon Foundation, a drug rehabilitation center in Santa Monica, and it took a three-year stay there for him to kick the habit. While he was there he made a recording, *Sounds of Synanon* (1962), with other hospitalized musicians. To their surprise, it was a hit and Joe won the *Downbeat* "New Star" award in 1963. After Synanon, he started working with George Shearing and made several critically acclaimed recordings during the mid-to-late 1960s, including *For Django* (1964) and *The Living Legends* (1969).

Joe's career really blossomed during the early 1970s. He continued to work with major jazz musicians during this period and, sometime in 1973, while playing at a club in Los Angeles, he was noticed by Norman Granz, owner of the newly-formed Pablo jazz label. Pass made many best-selling recordings for this label including *Virtuoso* (1973), *Virtuoso 2* (1976), and *Virtuoso 3* (1977). He also worked as a sideman for stellar jazz artists such as Oscar Peterson, Duke Ellington, Count Basie, and Ella Fitzgerald. Pass carried on playing jazz guitar right up until his death, from cancer, in 1994.

Joe Pass's fluid, lyrical soloing and advanced harmonic ideas owed much to his study of jazz horn players such as Charlie Parker. He is shown here onstage in Houston, Texas, in 1983.

Les Paul

b.1916

The name of Les Paul is inextricably linked to the history of the electric guitar, though his fame probably owes more to his technological innovations than it does to his undoubted six-string virtuosity: he helped to pioneer the concept of the electric solid body guitar and the Gibson Les Paul, named after him, became one of the most famous guitars in the world.

Lester William Polfus was born in Waukesha, Wisconsin, on June 9, 1916. Aged nine, he heard a street musician playing a harmonica and stared at the man until he was eventually given the instrument. It wasn't long before young Lester was himself proficient enough to play for money in the streets of Waukesha. By the age of 10 he was experimenting with sound, in one instance modifying the rolls of his mother's player piano, much to her annoyance. He started learning the guitar at the age of 11 and, by the time he was 18, was playing country music under the name Rhubarb Red. However, after hearing Django Reinhardt, he switched to jazz, changing his name to Les Paul. His inventive new guitar style caused a stir—he often featured humorous licks that delighted concert audiences—and he soon found himself playing with the likes of Nat King Cole and Bing Crosby, for whom Paul's light, warm sound provided a neat musical complement.

In an horrific car crash in 1948, Les's right arm was shattered almost beyond repair. When a doctor told him that he could set the arm in only one position, at which it would have to remain, Les told him to set it at an angle that allowed him to play guitar. He then went on to design a compact solid body guitar to suit his damaged arm and this led to Epiphone building a crude electric instrument called The Log, comprising a set of guitar strings fixed to part of a railroad sleeper; notes were sustained by the use of an amplifier. This in turn inspired the Gibson company to produce the first Gibson Les Paul guitars, which became hugely popular when blues-rock and pop artists started using them during the 1960s. The Gibson Les Paul remains one of the most popular guitar designs to this day.

Paul scored a number of hits during the 1950s, some featuring his future wife Mary Ford. Most of them highlighted his pioneering work with multitrack recording and his development of sound effects, such as reverb. Paul's recording career slowed down after the birth of rock and roll and he devoted much of the next 20 years to working on new recording techniques. Problems with his hearing prevented him from touring again until 1974, but three years later he recorded the Grammy-winning *Chester And Lester* with country legend Chet Atkins. Paul played regularly at Fat Tuesdays in New York during the 1980s, a decade during which he occasionally appeared alongside other guitar greats, including Jeff Beck. He also made an appearance at the Guitar Legends Seville Expo in Spain in 1992. After more than 60 years in the business, Les Paul continues to play guitar.

Les Paul's influence on the development of the modern electric guitar—both in his capacity as a gifted guitarist and as an inspired inventor—is incalculable. He is seen here in the 1950s.

Carl Perkins

1932–1998

Carl Perkins was born into a family of Tennessee sharecroppers; their poverty brought them into close contact with their African-American neighbors, whose music Carl absorbed throughout his childhood. He was taught to play guitar by an African-American farmworker, and passed on his skills to his brothers Jay and Clayton, who took up rhythm guitar and bass. In 1954, after making a name for himself as a singer, songwriter, and guitarist (backed by Jay and Clayton), Carl signed to Sun Records of Memphis, releasing several locally successful singles, and maintaining a busy schedule of gigs around Tennessee and its adjoining states. The group's music combined the sentiments and harmonies of white country music with a beat influenced by R&B and blues, producing the upbeat, dynamic music subsequently known as rockabilly. Perkins's urgent guitar-picking, a style similar to that of Chet Atkins and Merle Travis, fueled the driving sound of his group.

At a show in Amory, Mississippi, fellow Sun artist Johnny Cash suggested a song line to Carl: "Don't step on my blue suede shoes." Cash had overheard the phrase while on military service, and Perkins quickly worked it into a new number, "Blue Suede Shoes," which he recorded in December 1955. It became the first-ever single to reach the national, country, and R&B Top 5, making Carl's distinctive vocals and bold, rocking electric guitar immediately famous. Soon, he and his brothers were in demand all over the country. However, disaster struck in March 1956 when they were involved in a road accident en route to a TV appearance in New York. Carl and Jay were seriously injured; and during their convalescence, Elvis Presley began to promote his own version of "Blue Suede Shoes," effectively robbing Carl of the chance to capitalize on his initial success.

Carl Perkins never scored another comparable hit, though his follow-up singles for Sun, including "Dixie Fried" (1956) and "Matchbox" (1957), sold well. Sadly, his brother Jay died in 1958 after developing a brain tumor caused by his crash injuries and both Clayton (who committed suicide in 1974) and Carl himself subsequently became alcoholics. However, Perkins became an inspiration to many in the wave of British bands who dominated the rock and roll scene in the early to mid-1960s. The Beatles were huge Perkins fans, and covered three of his songs—"Honey Don't," "Matchbox," and "Everybody's Tryin' To Be My Baby"—early in their recording career.

Carl eventually conquered his drinking problem—primarily as a result of his strong religious faith—spent nine years as a sideman for Johnny Cash, and reached the country music charts on a number of occasions. He remained active as a performer throughout the rest of his life, often collaborating with the many famous names—including George Harrison and Paul McCartney—for whom his music had served as an inspiration.

Carl Perkins's guitar-picking, influenced by country music guitarists, did much to define the sound of rockabilly, from which rock and roll sprang. He is shown here during a 1964 U.K. tour.

Baden Powell

Baden Powell de Aquino was born in Rio de Janeiro, Brazil, on August 6, 1937. His father, himself a violinist and guitarist, was a Brazilian Boy Scouts leader who named his son after the British founder of the legendary movement. Baden started playing the guitar at the age of eight, stealing his first instrument from his aunt: "I was afraid to ask her," he recalled in later life, "I thought stealing easier." His instructor, Jaime Florence, taught him Brazilian popular tunes and classical pieces by Spanish guitarists Andrés Segovia and Francisco Tárrega, and also introduced him to the work of jazz guitarists such as Django Reinhardt and Barney Kessel. Baden proved to be a prodigy and won a music contest broadcast on Brazil's Rádio Nacional. By his midteens, he was almost making a living out of performing at balls and parties.

After leaving school, Baden worked for Rádio Nacional and also began composing songs. At this stage in his career, his primary influences were jazz and choro, a uniquely Brazilian form of instrumental music in which virtuoso performances and improvisation are key elements. (Powell's father regularly organized choro evenings, many of which were attended by saxophonist and flautist Pixinguinha, possibly the greatest choro musician of them all.) Baden's first success came with "Samba Triste" ("Sad Samba"), which he cowrote with lyricist Billy Blanco in 1956. Several years later, he met Vinícius de Moraes, a prominent poet and songwriter, and they collaborated on more than 50 songs, many of which are now firmly established in the bossa nova repertoire. During this period, Powell also worked with renowned composer Antonio Carlos Jobim, a prominent Brazilian jazz pioneer.

A six-month trip to Bahia, eastern Brazil, in 1964 introduced Baden to Afro-Brazilian culture and thereafter his guitar playing incorporated African rhythms along with jazz improvisations and classical harmonies. The resulting melting pot of musical styles, known as Afrosamba, revolutionized Brazilian samba music. Baden eschewed a clean sound in his playing, opting instead to strive for the feeling he heard in the sound of African percussion.

When Baden toured the U.S. and Europe during the 1960s, his superb technique and exquisite musicianship were received warmly. He had commercial and critical success with his first album, *Tristeza On Guitar* (1966), and went on to record many others including *Poems On Guitar* (1967), *Fresh Winds* (1969), *Solitude On Guitar* (1971), *The Frankfurt Opera Concert Live* (1975), *Melancolie* (1985), *Afro Sambas* (1996), and *A Vontade* (1997).

Baden was a major figure in the development of bossa nova and probably Brazil's foremost guitarist of the last half of the twentieth century, although, ironically, he remained better known in America and Europe than in his own country. He died from pneumonia on September 26, 2000.

Baden Powell's warm, jazz-tinged guitar playing drew on his knowledge of African music and classical guitar, and was a key element in the development of bossa nova in the 1960s.

Bonnie Raitt

b.1949

Raised in Los Angeles, Bonnie Raitt first became interested in folk music at summer camp when she was seven, and was given her first guitar the following Christmas. She later developed a passion for the blues, dropping out of college at Cambridge, Massachusetts, in 1969 to become a full-time performer, and making her initial impact with numerous live appearances around the nearby Boston folk and blues club scene.

During this period, she learned many of her musical skills directly from blues artists such as slide guitarist Fred McDowell, whom she visited at his Mississippi home to study his playing. The results of this dedication were soon reflected in the growing power and authority of her style. Country blues and R&B featured heavily on her debut LP, *Bonnie Raitt* (1971), which saw Raitt trade electric licks effortlessly with Chicago harmonica great Junior Wells. On its follow-up, *Give It Up* (1972), she offers sinuous acoustic guitar on "Love Me Like A Man," while "Give It Up Or Let Me Go" features her sweetly melodious resonator accompaniment.

Bonnie Raitt's other 1970s albums were similarly impressive, and featured a rich variety of material, including songs by Randy Newman and John Prine. In 1977, she enjoyed a modest hit single with a cover version of Del Shannon's "Runaway," but subsequent records sold less well. Raitt's career went through an uncertain phase in the mid-1980s, when she suffered from drink- and drug-related problems, culminating in her being dropped by her record company.

Above: Raitt has played slide since the late 1960s. No less a figure than B.B. King has called her "the best slide guitarist out there, bar none."

However, by the end of the decade, Bonnie Raitt was back in the studio, contributing to John Lee Hooker's acclaimed album *The Healer* (1990) and making a new album of her own, *Nick of Time*, which was released in 1989. Its highlights included the self-penned classic "The Road's My Middle Name," and the album became a U.S. number 1 best-seller and multiple Grammy winner. Raitt has gone on to achieve substantial success with more recent recordings, and has now finally achieved the widespread recognition her work has long deserved. Aside from playing, Raitt is also an active supporter of a range of charities, including the Rhythm and Blues Foundation, set up in 1988 to provide financial and medical assistance to veteran performers.

Left: Bonnie Raitt, seen here during a live performance early in her career, has established herself as the best-known female guitar virtuoso in rock and blues.

Ernest Ranglin

b.1932

Ernest Ranglin was born in Manchester, Jamaica, on June 19, 1932. He started playing the ukulele as a young boy and had progressed to the guitar by the time he was a teenager, teaching himself to play from guitar books, and by listening to Charlie Christian records. He joined his first band, the Val Bennett Orchestra, in 1948, and his reputation grew until he was snapped up three years later by the Eric Deans Orchestra, Jamaica's most popular group at the time. They toured around the Caribbean and Bahamas during the 1950s, playing tunes by Benny Goodman and Duke Ellington. Jazz has remained Ranglin's first love throughout his long career, during which his long melodic lines, crisp timing, and ear for harmonic progressions have become highly respected.

In 1959, Ernest joined forces with Chris Blackwell, a record producer, and studio group Clue J & His Blues Blasters. They developed a unique new sound and recorded a tune, "Shuffling Jug," that is now regarded as one of the earliest examples of ska, a popular 1960s music style that later gave birth to reggae and ragga music. Ranglin's guitar came to more or less define the ska rhythm that would be heard on subsequent Jamaican releases—Ranglin himself claims that about 80 percent of the releases from Jamaica's famous Studio One recording studio feature him on guitar.

Blackwell went to England in 1962 to launch his own record label, Island Records. He invited Ranglin and Millie Small, a Jamaican singer, over there to record what turned out to be a worldwide hit single—"My Boy Lollipop." Ernest was also an accomplished jazz guitarist and, with his own quintet, he recorded two albums during the mid-1960s: *Wranglin'* (1964) and *Reflections* (1965). His versatility and unique musicianship meant he was in constant demand both as a ska musician and as a jazz guitar player. Ronnie Scott, owner of London's premier jazz club, was so impressed by Ranglin's musicianship when the guitarist played in his club in 1964, that he invited him to become resident guitarist, a position Ranglin occupied for the next nine months.

During the 1970s and 1980s, Ernest recorded two more albums: *Ranglin' Roots* (1977) and *From Kingston To Miami* (1982). He resumed his passion for jazz during the 1990s, playing at the 1995 Montreux Jazz Festival with pianist Monty Alexander, and at the 1996 Barbados Jazz Festival with singer, composer, and arranger Ray Charles. He continued into the millennium with *Modern Answers To Old Problems* (2000), an adventurous mix of jazz and Afro-pop, and a follow-up album, *Gotcha!* (2001), continued in this eclectic direction. Today, Ranglin is widely recognized both as a pioneering force behind modern Caribbean music and as a uniquely talented jazz guitar player.

Despite his primary role in the evolution of ska, Ernest Ranglin thinks of himself as a jazz musician above all. "Ska is pop music and cannot be compared to jazz," he insists. "Jazz is better than classical music, because you are creating it every time you play."

Django Reinhardt

1910–1953

Django Reinhardt was a phenomenon. He was a legend in his own time and that legendary status seems even greater now, nearly 50 years after his death. His lyrical solos and exciting rhythm work have inspired generations of musicians and his compositions rank among some of the very best for acoustic guitar. Few jazz guitar fans around the world do not have at least one Django Reinhardt record in their collection.

Jean Baptiste (Django) Reinhardt was born into a nomadic gypsy family in Belgium on January 23, 1910. He showed an early interest in music and, by his mid-teens, was proficient on the guitar, banjo, and violin. As a young man he settled in Paris, where he discovered American jazz and subsequently made a living in the city as a street musician. However, tragedy struck when he was just 18: he lost the use of two fingers in his left hand after an horrific caravan fire. For most guitarists this would have meant the end of a musical career; Reinhardt not only overcame the disability but also developed a new, unique way of playing the guitar, delivering astonishing solos with just the first two fingers of his left hand. He reputedly played with such force that he wore out a guitar every six months.

Above: Reinhardt's solos were played with only two fingers, and often on a single string.

In 1933, Reinhardt formed the Quintette du Hot Club de France with violinist Stephane Grappelli, brother Joseph Reinhardt and Roger Chaput on guitars, and Louis Vola on bass. They recorded more than 100 songs and became internationally famous. The band's sound was dominated by Reinhardt's lyrical swing and the melodic interplay between his guitar and Grappelli's violin, and was to become a huge influence on the next generation of jazz guitarists all over the world. The quintet's most famous tune, "Nuages," reached the hit parade in many countries during the late 1940s and it is considered by many to be one of the most memorable tunes from this period.

Reinhardt died of a stroke in May 1953, after an afternoon of fishing on the bank of the river Seine. He left behind a rich heritage of guitar music that continues to astound and delight musicians and music lovers all over the world.

Left: Suaveness itself—Django Reinhardt, photographed during the late 1940s. Technically outstanding and a superb improviser, Reinhardt was Europe's first truly great jazz musician.

John Renbourn

b.1944

John Renbourn was born in London, and studied classical guitar and Early Music as a teenager before becoming involved in the skiffle boom sweeping the U.K. in the late 1950s. Like thousands of his contemporaries, he started out by copying American folk and blues players, but soon developed a more eclectic approach, taking in elements of the English medieval and Renaissance music he had heard at school, as well as the R&B he picked up while playing electric guitar in a band at Kingston College of Art, southwest of London.

Reverting to acoustic guitar, Renbourn joined London's growing folk scene, which included established figures such as Davy Graham and recent arrivals like Bert Jansch (the young Scottish guitarist who became John's roommate); Jansch guested on his first solo LP, *John Renbourn* (1965). The following year, the two players came together again for *Bert And John*, recorded, like several of their early efforts, on primitive equipment in the broom cupboard of their London apartment and epitomizing the "folk-baroque" style that they have both been credited with shaping. Renbourn, perhaps the more melodic of the two, contributed intricate lines and rich harmonies, while Jansch provided much of the rhythmic drive—though on some arrangements, the parts are too tightly interwoven to permit such distinctions.

By 1966, Renbourn and Jansch were performing regularly with singer Jacqui McShee—with whom Renbourn collaborated on the acclaimed *Another Day* the following year—and were sometimes joined by drummer Terry Cox and string bassist Danny Thompson. This ad hoc ensemble evolved into Pentangle, a folk group at heart that also incorporated elements of blues and jazz into its music. Pentangle toured widely over the next few years, appearing at prestigious venues such as Carnegie Hall and taking in the Newport Folk Festival and the 1970 Isle of Wight Festival. Pentangle's concerts and recording commitments were to absorb much of Renbourn's time and energy for the next few years. After the band's break-up in 1973, he continued to work with McShee and other long-standing musical associates in The John Renbourn Group, which issued two studio albums, and received a Grammy nomination for the 1982 LP *Live In America*, recorded at San Francisco's Great American Music Hall.

At around this time, Renbourn cut back on live gigs while taking a three-year course in composition and orchestration at the renowned Dartington music college in southwest England, but he has subsequently been performing and recording in a wide range of contexts—notably with former Incredible String Band member Robin Williamson. His most recent solo CD, *Traveller's Prayer*, appeared in 1999 and saw Renbourn combine traditional themes with unconventional arrangements, to widespread acclaim.

John Renbourn, shown here in 1993, is one of England's finest folk-inspired guitarists, but has also drawn on medieval music, blues, jazz, and Eastern influences during his long career.

Keith Richards

b.1943

To fans and detractors alike, Keith Richards personifies the rock and roll lifestyle in all its rebelliousness, hedonism, and excess. But Richards's wild and dangerous image has often obscured the true reason for his enduring fame: the raunchy, instantly recognizable guitar playing that has been the bedrock of The Rolling Stones' sound since the 1960s.

A devotee of Elvis Presley, Chuck Berry, and Chicago blues, Keith Richards grew up within a few miles of Mick Jagger in the county of Kent, to the southeast of London. After meeting as children, Mick and Keith lost touch, but in 1960 the two met again by chance on a train. They were soon enthusiastically discussing their mutual love of R&B, particularly those artists who recorded for the Chess label. Before long, Richards had joined a group in which Jagger was then singing, Little Boy Blue & The Blue Boys. Over the next two years, Jagger and Richards gained experience and exposure on the London blues scene, from which they would subsequently pluck Brian Jones, Billy Wyman, and Charlie Watts to form The Rolling Stones.

The Stones' early chart successes were R&B cover versions of tracks such as Chuck Berry's "Come On," Buddy Holly's "Not Fade Away," and The Beatles' "I Wanna Be Your Man"; a remake of The Valentinos' "It's All Over Now" gave the group their first U.K. number 1. By the mid-1960s, however, Jagger and Richards were composing the band's hits, and Keith's strident, powerful playing—epitomized by his classic riff for "Satisfaction" (1965)—was starting to dominate their sound. He was also experimenting with the open blues tunings that would soon become a key feature of his style. These were first showcased on *Beggars Banquet* (1968), but it was at the sessions for *Let It Bleed* (1969) and the single "Honky Tonk Women" (1969) that Ry Cooder introduced Richards to the open G tuning (D G D G B D) that he subsequently made his own. Unlike Cooder, however, Richards found that the bass D string inhibited his technique, and since the early 1970s, most of his instruments, including the Fender Telecasters he uses onstage, have been fitted with just five strings.

In recent years, the Stones' music has not always managed to equal the excitement of their 1960s heyday, or subsequent guitar-driven hits such as "Brown Sugar" (1971) and "It's Only Rock 'N' Roll" (1974), but Richards has continued to come up with some superb songs and guitar parts. The visceral introduction to "Start Me Up" (1981) ranks among his most memorable achievements, while "Undercover Of The Night" (1983) boasted some classic Richards riffing, simultaneously biting and funky. His solo career has also earned him plaudits. Richards's 1992 solo LP, *Main Offender,* earned a somewhat two-edged accolade from one music critic: "the best Stones album in 17 years."

The man they call "the human riff." Keith Richards onstage at the Oshawa Civic Auditorium, Canada, during the late 1970s.

Cesar Rosas

b.1954

Born in Los Angeles, Cesar Rosas played electric guitar in rock bands throughout his teenage years, developing a fiery style that owed much to the energy of early rock and roll. However, after leaving school, he and his friends, singer-guitarist and accordionist David Hidalgo, bassist Conrad Lozano, and drummer Louie Perez, became fascinated by traditional Mexican music and formed Los Lobos del Este de Los Angeles (The Wolves of East L.A.) in 1973. Initially, the quartet was entirely acoustic, but by the early 1980s Rosas and Hidalgo were using electric guitars; and in 1982, they added a fifth member, saxophonist Steve Berlin, to further expand their sound.

Rechristening themselves Los Lobos, the group released a Grammy award-winning EP, ...*And A Time To Dance*, in 1983. The following year, their LP *How Will the Wolf Survive?*, which featured a heady mix of influences including Tex-Mex, folk, blues, jazz, and rock and roll, brought them national chart success. The album also demonstrates the full power and versatility of Rosas's electric guitar playing: he provides most of the lead parts for Los Lobos, and dominates "Don't Worry Baby" (on which he provides meaty riffing that reflects his long-standing love of R&B), while sounding equally at home on the two-beat polka-style rhythms of "Corrido #1" and "Serenata Nortena."

By The Light of the Moon, issued in early 1987, contained a similarly winning combination of Mexican music and rock, although commercial success still seemed a long way off for the band. However, all that was to change in the summer of 1987, when the group's version of Ritchie Valens's "La Bamba" reached number 1 in the U.S. and U.K. (The song was taken from a film about Valens released that year.) Cesar Rosas's reactions to this chart-topping single were ambivalent. He later explained that, "We didn't want to get typecast as a La Bamba sort of band," and Los Lobos' next record, *La Pistola Y El Corazón* (1988), was a defiantly anticommercial (but critically acclaimed) acoustic album of Mexican folk material, which secured the band its second Grammy award.

Subsequent CDs have continued to reflect the group's eclecticism and versatility, although in recent years, its members have been increasingly involved in side projects. Rosas and Hidalgo have appeared alongside Tex-Mex stars such as accordionist Flaco Jimenez in Los Super Seven (which they describe as "a Latin Traveling Wilburys"), and in 1999, Cesar released his first solo album, *Soul Disguise*. The album is a showcase for Rosas's vocal and instrumental skills. He turns in some especially impressive playing on an echo-laden version of Ike Turner's "You've Got To Lose" and his own "Little Heaven," while his use of wild wah-wah, distortion, and feedback elsewhere on the record are testament to his affection for high-energy rock and roll.

Cesar Rosas's guitar playing draws heavily on both Tex-Mex and 1950s rock. He is shown here during the making of the video for Los Lobos' breakthrough 1987 hit "La Bamba."

Carlos Santana

b.1947

Carlos Santana grew up in the Mexican city of Tijuana; his father was a traditional mariachi violinist, but Carlos was more interested in learning the blues, and was already playing B.B. King-influenced guitar before he moved to the U.S. in 1961. His new home was in San Francisco, where he became part of the thriving cultural scene that spawned The Grateful Dead and other major groups; and in 1966, he assembled the first lineup of The Santana Blues Band—later to be known simply by its founder's surname.

By 1969, the group's blend of psychedelia, blues, and Latin styles, and Carlos's searing, soaring lead guitar lines (as showcased on tracks such as "Soul Sacrifice" from the band's debut album *Santana*, issued that year) were attracting a large audience. Their career was given a further boost when they made a triumphant appearance at the Woodstock Festival that summer, highlighted by Carlos's effusive guitar playing and the scintillating drumming of 16-year-old Michael Shrieve. Subsequently, *Santana* reached number 4 on the U.S. album charts, earning a gold disk. The band's second album, *Abraxas* (1970), with Carlos excelling on a powerful reworking of Peter Green's "Black Magic Woman" and Tito Puente's "Oye Como Va" (both hit singles), topped the U.S. charts and was a multi-million seller. However, there were growing tensions within the band, which split up in 1971 after the release of a highly acclaimed third album, and subsequent incarnations of the group were marked by frequent personnel changes. This did little to affect the quality of the music: *Caravanserai* (1972) saw Carlos add a new keyboardist and percussionist and embrace a more free, jazz-oriented direction to stunning effect.

Carlos himself has pursued many nonband-related projects, including the albums *Love Devotion Surrender* (1973) with fellow guitarist virtuoso John McLaughlin, and *The Swing Of Delight* (1980) with keyboardist Herbie Hancock and saxophonist Wayne Shorter. He has also collaborated with Bob Dylan and John Lee Hooker. In 1986, Carlos produced the soundtrack for the Richie Valens biopic, *La Bamba*. However, he has always remained committed to his group, whose records and tours enjoyed consistent success throughout the 1980s and 1990s, but never seemed likely to regain the massive popularity of their early days.

This situation was changed dramatically by the release of *Supernatural* in 1999. The album skillfully combines Santana's classic sound with contributions from contemporary stars such as vocalists Lauryn Hill and Matchbox 20's Rob Thomas (who co-wrote the hit single "Smooth"). The album also features a guest appearance by Eric Clapton. Carlos's own playing is as fresh as ever on "Corazon Espinado" and "(da le) Yaleo"; worldwide sales of the disk have now topped 21 million copies.

With a style characterized by sustained notes and sinuous, molten runs of notes, Carlos Santana is responsible for some of the most sensuous guitar playing in rock music.

John Scofield

John Scofield was born in Dayton, Ohio, but grew up in Wilton, Connecticut, where he developed an affection for blues and rock and roll. He first picked up the guitar at the age of 12, but it wasn't until he was 15, when he took jazz lessons with a local teacher, that he started practicing in earnest. As a teenager, Scofield played R&B, urban blues, soul, and rock and roll in local groups. Soon, however, he became fascinated by jazz guitar, and quickly absorbed the styles of Wes Montgomery, Tal Farlow, Barney Kessel, and Jim Hall, all prominent jazz players during the 1960s.

Scofield left high school in 1970 and moved to Boston to study jazz at the Berklee School of Music with Jim Hall and Mick Goodrick, both big names in the jazz guitar world at the time. His first break as a musician came in the form of professional work with vibraphone player Gary Burton, another Berklee teacher. Scofield's career received another vital boost when, at Mick Goodrick's recommendation, he was invited to play in a band led by saxophonist Gerry Mulligan and trumpeter Chet Baker at a Carnegie Hall concert. Scofield's playing soon attracted attention from others and he was asked to join drummer Billy Cobham's jazz-rock group in 1975. He also worked with the celebrated jazz bass player Charles Mingus and keyboardist George Duke during the late 1970s.

Shortly after recording a solo album, *Shinola* (1982), Scofield joined trumpeter Miles Davis's band. Miles always had the uncanny ability of making his musicians play to the very best of their abilities and Scofield was no exception to the rule. During the three years he was with Davis, his musical voice blossomed. He developed a unique guitar style characterized by original blues-style licks and unusual, across-the-beat phrasing. He later recalled, "My stint with Miles made me sure that there really was a kind of music that was both funky and improvised at the same time." This cross-pollination of funk and improvisatory jazz was even more evident on some of the excellent recordings he made with his own band during the 1980s: *Electric Outlet* (1984), the funky *Still Warm* (1986), *Blue Matter* (1987), and *Loud Jazz* (1988). All of these releases revealed a character and drive that had been lacking in his 1982 recording.

Over the years, Scofield's guitar playing has matured even further and he has produced a string of original, critically acclaimed jazz albums including *Time On My Hands* (1990), *Hand Jive* (1994), the exceptional Gil Evans-influenced *Quiet* (1996), and *A Go Go* (1998). He has also played and recorded with many other top jazz musicians, including guitarists Pat Metheny, Bill Frisell, and John Abercrombie, bass players Steve Swallow and Charlie Haden, and drummers Dennis Chambers and Jack DeJohnette.

John Scofield's musical education, including three vital years with Miles Davis's band, has given the guitarist an exceptionally broad jazz palette. Scofield plays both electric and acoustic guitar in a distinctive style that incorporates bebop, funk, country, and blues.

Andrés Segovia

1893–1987

Andrés Segovia holds a unique place in the history of the Spanish guitar. He revolutionized the instrument's playing style, assembled its basic repertoire, and established and sustained its popularity during more than 60 years of concert recitals and recording.

Segovia was born and brought up in Andalucía, southern Spain, but took an early dislike to the region's traditional flamenco style of guitar-playing. Preferring a more formal musical approach, he taught himself to play the guitar; his family was opposed to Segovia's musical aspirations—the guitar was not regarded as a particularly respectable instrument at the time—and denied him a tutor. His early studies included guitar pieces by various Spanish composers (including Francisco Tárrega, known as "the Chopin of the guitar") as well as transcriptions of piano and string works. Segovia made his professional debut at Granada in 1909, and his fame grew rapidly after later appearances in Madrid and Barcelona—despite controversy over his use of fingernails to strike the instrument's strings. Most previous guitarists had plucked the strings with their fingertips, but Segovia's self-developed technique (now considered the norm for classical players) produced a clearer, richer sound and greater volume. Its expressive possibilities quickly inspired a host of new guitar works dedicated to the young virtuoso, among them compositions by Federico Moreno Torroba, Manuel de Falla, Manuel Ponce, and Heitor Villa-Lobos.

Soon, Segovia was appearing all over Europe and South America, and touring the U.S. and the Far East, a demanding playing schedule that he was to maintain for the rest of his life. He confined his tours to North and South America during World War II, but resumed global touring thereafter. Segovia's recitals usually featured both original compositions and transcriptions, and he succeeded in gaining acceptance for the guitar among serious musicians by including established masterpieces, including works by J.S. Bach, Handel, Mozart, Haydn, Schumann, and Chopin, in his programs. He strove tirelessly to promote the classical instrument via his own books, broadcasts, and records, and also safeguarded its future by encouraging and tutoring emerging performers via his master class courses in Santiago de Compostela, Spain; Siena, Italy; and Berkeley, California. His many distinguished pupils included John Williams, Julian Bream, Alirio Diaz, and Oscar Ghilia.

Segovia was scornful of folk and popular playing styles, and had little time for the more radical trends of twentieth-century music, but such opinions were part of the single-mindedness and strength of purpose that characterized his long and extraordinary career.

Segovia's determined efforts saw the guitar gain a respectability as a classical instrument that it had not previously possessed. He is seen here in Granada in the early 1950s.

Johnny Smith

b.1922

Although he is best known for his 1952 hit "Moonlight In Vermont," Johnny Smith is also widely respected as an exceptional guitarist who influenced several generations of guitar players. To many, he is as crucial an early influence as Charlie Christian.

John Henry Smith Jr. was born in Birmingham, Alabama on June 25, 1922. He started playing the trumpet, violin, and guitar at an early age. When work dried up in Birmingham during the Depression, the Smiths moved through a series of cities, ending up in Maine. Here, Johnny struck an enterprising deal with local pawn shops: they would allow him to practice on any guitars they had as long as he tuned the instruments for them! By the time he was 15, Smith had become an accomplished musician, and was soon playing in a hillbilly band, Uncle Lem and the Mountain Boys. However, he was also increasingly attracted to the freedom and spontaneity of jazz and in 1940 he formed his own jazz combo.

After spending the war playing in Air Corps bands (imperfect vision prevented him from flying), Smith settled in New York, where he took up a position as staff musician and arranger with NBC. It was there that he met saxophonist Stan Getz and the two recorded "Moonlight In Vermont," a piece that established Smith as a major jazz talent. In his heyday, Smith had a unique, quiet style of playing that epitomized the term "cool jazz." His exceptional, rapid single-note runs, complex chord variations, and tasteful harmonies dominated "Moonlight In Vermont" and several subsequent albums recorded for Roost Records during the 1950s and early 1960s, including *Johnny Smith Quintet* (1952), *In a Sentimental Mood* (1954), *The New Johnny Smith Quartet* (1956), *Favorites* (1959), and the critically acclaimed *Man With The Blue Guitar* (1962).

Smith's versatility enabled him to work in a number of different musical genres from the late 1940s onward, and saw him secure positions with both the New York Philharmonic and the Philadelphia Symphony Orchestras. Jazz remained his true love, however. From the early 1950s on, he regularly appeared at the famous jazz club Birdland with his own quintet, featuring Getz, sharing bills with the likes of Dizzie Gillespie, Thelonious Monk, and Charlie Parker. The Gibson guitar company was impressed enough by Smith's playing to bring out a special Johnny Smith archtop model in 1960.

In 1963, Johnny opened a specialist guitar store in Colorado Springs. He continued to play at local jazz clubs and recorded *Reminiscing* (1965) with local musicians but, despite further album releases, his interest in performing waned. He has been professionally retired for some time, but appeared as a judge at the 1996 International Jazz Guitar Competition in Nashville, where the top prize was a Johnny Smith model guitar.

Johnny Smith's formidable technique encompassed speedy single-note solos, inspired chord changes, and acute harmonic awareness, while his understated rhythm work highlighted the guitar's value as an accompanying instrument. He is shown here with a Johnny Smith Gibson.

Martin Taylor

b.1956

Martin Taylor was born in Harlow, England, on October 20, 1956. He began to play a half-sized guitar at the very early age of four. Martin's father, also a musician, introduced him to the early recordings of Eddie Lang, Django Reinhardt, Carl Kress, and Ike Isaacs and, by the time he was 12, Martin was a proficient jazz guitar player and already owned his first electric guitar, a Guild Starfire. Although the jazz guitar greats had an enormous influence on his playing style, Martin also listened long and hard to keyboard legends such as Art Tatum and Bill Evans. He became intrigued by the fact that piano players were able to be self-contained musicians, providing rhythm, background, and solo parts. Martin's natural musical talent, combined with his total dedication to his instrument (he is entirely self-taught), soon started paying off: he left school at 15 because he already had a full-time gig schedule.

During the early 1970s, Martin worked with the Lennie Hastings Band and the Harry Bence Band. He also formed a celebrated guitar duo with Ike Isaacs. It was during this time that he began to develop a formidable right-hand fingerstyle technique that has enabled him to get a full sound out of the guitar without any accompaniment, recalling his early fascination with the self-contained nature of piano playing. (His powerful playing style comes at a cost, however: Martin finds that most sets of strings only last him for one gig!) Some of these skills were displayed on his debut solo album, *Taylor Made* (1979). He joined Stephane Grappelli's quartet in 1979 and subsequently played all over the world with the legendary violinist. They made several noted recordings including *At The Winery* (1980) and *Vintage 1981* (1981), and played for radio and TV broadcasts on both sides of the Atlantic. During the 1980s, he also toured with other guitarists such as Louis Stewart and the late Emily Remler, and other noted musicians including Peter King (saxophone) and Buddy De Franco (clarinet). He even appeared with Barney Kessel and Charlie Byrd in a later incarnation of their famous Great Guitars group; he has also played with a number of rock musicians, including Eric Clapton, Peter Frampton, and Yes guitarist Steve Howe. Around this time, Taylor made a number of recordings of his own including *Skye Boat* (1981), *Sketches—A Tribute To Art Tatum* (1978 and 1982), and *Sarabanda* (1988), although it was not until 1986 that he performed his first solo concert.

Martin's reputation became even greater during the 1990s and his later recordings *Don't Fret* (1990), *Artistry* (1992), *Spirit Of Django* (1994), and *Portraits* (1995) have showcased his outstanding musicianship and phenomenal right-hand technique. He was once described by the late, great country player Chet Atkins as "One of the greatest and most impressive guitarists in the world today"—high praise indeed.

Martin Taylor's fluid and strongly melodic guitar playing has accompanied some of the finest musicians in the world, including Stephane Grappelli, Yehudi Menuhin, and Kenny Burrell.

Ali Farka Toure

b.1939

For many years, musicologists have theorized about the West African roots of the blues, but a single song by Malian guitarist Ali Farka Toure demonstrates the connection more clearly than any academic treatise could. Toure's lyrics may be in an unfamiliar language, but his voice and playing style strike an immediate chord with anyone who has heard John Lee Hooker or Lightnin' Hopkins. Moreover, his music's ability to communicate across cultures, as well as its extraordinary richness and subtlety, have made him by far the best-known African guitarist in America and Europe.

Toure still lives in Niafunke, the village in the Timbuktu region of Northern Mali where he spent much of his childhood. From an early age he played traditional instruments, such as the gurkel, a one-stringed instrument that he played during certain ceremonies and which is said to have a spiritual side to it. Toure only became interested in the guitar in 1956, after attending a performance by the National Ballet of Guinea, whose director, Keita Fodeba, used guitar to accompany his dancers. Toure subsequently became (in his own words) "a fool for the guitar," practicing obsessively and applying his existing musical knowledge to develop his own distinctive sound, characterized by a rhythmic picking, accompanied by his own, somewhat nasal vocals. During the early 1960s, Toure played with a local cultural troupe, but also started listening to American R&B and soul—Albert King, Otis Redding and, in particular, John Lee Hooker, made a big impression on the young West African. In the early 1970s, he was to play with John Lee Hooker in Paris; fittingly, the celebrated bluesman announced that Toure was his natural successor.

Ali's achievements as a guitarist and singer later made him famous throughout West Africa, but despite occasional overseas appearances (he undertook his first trip outside Africa in 1968) he remained relatively obscure elsewhere until he began to tour more widely in the 1980s. His all-acoustic CD, *Ali Farka Toure*, recorded on a visit to London in 1987, gave his profile a substantial boost; but the record that brought him major recognition in the U.S. was *Talking Timbuktu* (1994), a best-selling, Grammy-winning collaboration with Ry Cooder, whose slide-guitar work contributed eloquently to what critic Derek Rath described as "a super world summit without barriers or borders."

Since *Talking Timbuktu*, however, Toure has shown where his priorities lie. Running his farm in Mali and supporting his relatives there (he was born into a noble family and takes his duties to them very seriously) have always been more important to him than the life of a musician, and he has shown little inclination to resume extensive international concert-giving. Significantly, his latest album, *Niafunke* (1999), on which he is accompanied by local musicians, is named for his home village, and was recorded on location there.

Ali Farka Toure is one of the most respected world music guitarists. His unique combination of blues and West African music has earned him the nickname of "Bluesman of Africa."

Merle Travis

Raised in the coal mining area of Muhlenberg County, Kentucky, the first instrument Merle Travis learned to play was the banjo. Taking up guitar at the age of 12, he began to develop what later became known as "Travis picking," a method of striking the strings with the thumb and forefinger, derived from the banjo technique in use around his home region. By 1937 he was working in Louisville as guitarist and singer with fiddler Clayton McMichen's string band, The Georgia Wildcats. Soon afterward, he moved to Cincinnati, Ohio, where his broadcasts on station WLW were heard across several neighboring states, and he recorded with leading country artists such as Grandpa Jones.

During a brief spell in the U.S. Marines, Travis was posted to California. After his discharge in 1944, he settled in Los Angeles, becoming widely known for his appearances with broadcaster and musician Cliffie Stone on radio shows such as "Hollywood Barn Dance" and "Harmony Homestead." In 1946, Stone joined Capitol Records as an A&R man, and signed Travis to the label, where he enjoyed a string of successful singles, including "Divorce Me C.O.D." (1946) and "So Round, So Firm, So Fully Packed" (1947). Another song from this period, "Sixteen Tons," based on his childhood memories of Kentucky coal mining, was later a major hit for Tennessee Ernie Ford. Travis also cowrote Capitol Records' first million-seller, "Smoke, Smoke, Smoke That Cigarette"; he penned the song with Tex Williams, who sang on the hit recording. Several of Travis's songs featured quirky titles or subject matter, and this trait extended to his guitar playing: as part of his stage act at the time, Travis used his instrument to mimic animal sounds.

As well as his more commercial records, Travis made several largely instrumental LPs for Capitol, such as *Walkin' The Strings* (1960)—a breathtaking display of the possibilities of two-digit picking, containing an all-acoustic mixture of rags, blues, and other pieces that have inspired and challenged countless subsequent performers. Travis was also one of the first artists to use a solid-bodied, electric model, which he designed himself in the late 1940s. "I got the idea from a steel guitar," he once explained. "I wanted the same sustainability of notes, and I came up with a solid-body electric guitar with the keys all on one side." The instrument was built for Travis by his friend Paul Bigsby, and was thought by some to have influenced Leo Fender, creator of the Fender Telecaster and Stratocaster.

Despite alcohol-related problems that affected his career in the 1950s and 1960s, Merle Travis remained an important and highly respected figure in musical circles. He continued to be active as a performer until his death on October 20, 1983.

Merle Travis's influence as a guitarist is considerable. Not only did he develop the "Travis picking" style, later adopted by country stars including Doc Watson and Chet Atkins, but he also came up with the blueprint for a solid-bodied electric guitar.

Steve Vai

b.1960

Steve Vai was born in Long Island, New York, and started learning the guitar in his teens, taking lessons from another young player bound for future stardom, Joe Satriani. Vai continued his musical education at the prestigious Berklee School of Music in Boston, Massachusetts, where he broadened his musical palette by studying classical music and jazz. In 1980, he moved to Los Angeles to work as a sideman for Frank Zappa. Their association began with Vai's studio contributions to *You Are What You Is* (1981); and Steve made his live debut with Zappa's band on their 1980 U.S. tour, which was recorded live and released as *Tinseltown Rebellion* (1981).

Vai collaborated with Zappa during the next three years, becoming the subject of one of Frank's typically lewd lampoons in the song "Stevie's Spanking" (1984), to which Vai was brave enough to add a solo! However, Zappa left little doubt about the esteem in which he held the young musician: on the sleeve for the 1982 album *Ship Arriving Too Late To Save A Drowning Witch*, he refers to Vai as "stunt guitarist." Vai used the fees earned during this period for the down payment on a house where he installed a studio and recorded his first solo album, *Flex-Able* (1984), which clearly showed the influence of Satriani. The album sold steadily throughout the U.S. and Europe, receiving a further boost when Vai started to work with leading hard rock acts such as David Lee Roth and Whitesnake later in the decade. However, throughout the late 1980s he had also been working on a new solo album, *Passion & Warfare*, and it was this record that was to provide him with his real breakthrough. Released in 1990, the album saw Vai meld jazz, classical, funk, and hard rock and provided a spectacular showcase for his formidable playing skills. Tracks such as "Erotic Nightmares" display many of Vai's trademarks—lightning speed, leaping themes using the full compass of his specially developed seven-string Ibanez electric, and dramatic whammy bar bends—but he deploys his virtuoso technique with taste and sensitivity, and also proved himself capable of beautifully sustained, melodic soloing.

Passion & Warfare became a million seller, and Vai's career has subsequently gone from strength to strength. The guitarist released a compilation of his instrumental ballads in the fall of 2000, entitled *The 7th Song: Enchanting Guitar Melodies, Archives Vol. 1*. As well as making several further outstanding solo albums, he has recently been working with his former teacher Satriani on their ongoing G3 project: a series of tours in which Vai, Satriani, and, originally, Eric Johnson (subsequent replacements for the latter have included John Petrucci of Dream Theater) perform solo sets, and conclude each show by appearing together.

Steve Vai's stunning guitar pyrotechnics are complemented by a strong melodic sensibility that draws on his interest in classical music and jazz as well as straight-ahead rock and metal.

George Van Eps

1913–1998

As a child in New Jersey, George Van Eps grew up surrounded by music. His brothers Bobby, Freddy, and John played piano, trumpet, and sax respectively. George's father Fred was a respected banjo player who had recorded ragtime music on cylinders back in the 1890s, and his mother was a versatile pianist. His parents gave George a banjo one morning when he was nine and bedridden with juvenile rheumatoid arthritis, and returned that evening to discover him playing "Somebody Stole My Girl" and "Alabama Bound." His illness passed, although a doctor told his mother that George's heart was so weak he was not likely to live beyond 20. Determined to waste no time, George worked ceaselessly on his musicianship and was making recordings and playing in clubs by the time he was 14.

After hearing Eddie Lang's pioneering jazz guitar efforts, George switched over to the guitar during the early 1930s, and secured his first big musical break with Benny Goodman's orchestra in 1934. He later toured with pianist Ray Noble and carried out a stream of radio and studio engagements.

George's appetite for expanding the boundaries of guitar playing stemmed in part from his desire to emulate a pianist's ability to play melody, bass, and chords, all at the same time. During the mid-1930s, George started to develop his own, unique technique that would enable him to do the same thing on his guitar, which he frequently referred to as a "lap piano." The six-string guitar proved to have its limitations, so he designed a seven-string model with a low A-string and eventually persuaded the Epiphone guitar company to make him one. This adaptation helped expand his range greatly and he immediately became able to play richer, fuller arrangements, helped in part by his preference for working with chord progressions rather than opting for single-note solos. "I don't care about playing nine million notes a second," he once explained. "I'm more interested in having every voice in a chord be a melody that both stands by itself and works with the others." His new style matured over the years and he later made a number of milestone seven-string guitar recordings, including *Mellow Guitar* (1956), *My Guitar* (1965), *George Van Eps Seven String Guitar* (1967), *Soliloquy* (1968), *Hand-Crafted Swing* (1991), and *Keepin' Time* (1994). The success of these recordings inspired Epiphone to produce seven-string Les Paul Classic and Korina Flying V guitars.

Widely respected as a genuine pioneer of jazz guitar, George's incredible technique inspired later jazz greats such as Joe Pass and Wes Montgomery, and the range of his seven-string playing encouraged other notable players such as Howard Alden, Bucky Pizzarelli, and Ted Greene to play similar instruments. Van Eps was also a great teacher who coached and inspired more than four generations of guitar players.

Master of the seven-string guitar. George Van Eps's awesome technique enabled him to combine melody, chordal progressions, bass parts, and rhythm in the manner of a pianist.

Eddie Van Halen

b.1955

Edward Van Halen was born in the Netherlands; he and his family moved to the U.S. in 1962, settling in Pasadena, California. Both Edward and his brother Alex were musicians, following in the footsteps of their sax-playing father, and soon began to perform together at school and at home. Initially, Alex studied guitar while Edward learned drums, but they soon swapped instruments, and within a few years of launching their first serious rock band in 1971, they were working with bassist Michael Anthony and singer David Lee Roth in the band Mammoth—shortly to be renamed Van Halen.

By the mid-1970s, interest was growing in Eddie's remarkable guitar playing. His mastery of extreme whammy bar effects and the overall speed and control of his technique inspired superlatives from audiences and critics alike. Eddie's use of both his left and right hands to strike the strings—a technique known as "tapping"—became an early trademark. By hammering on one string with fingers on his left hand and sliding the pinky finger of his right hand along the same string, Eddie was able to create unusual harmonics. Until about 1977, he usually performed this trick with his back to the audience so as to preserve an air of mystery around how he created such a remarkable sound.

Eddie and the band were heard on record for the first time when Van Halen's self-titled debut album appeared in 1978. It spawned two hit singles, but its most influential track was "Eruption," on which Eddie demonstrated his instrumental prowess in a brief, toccatalike piece, culminating in a distorted assault on his low E string. The song became a highlight of Van Halen concerts and was extended into a showcase for the guitarist. Such guitar wizardry soon earned Eddie a reputation as being one of the hottest rock guitarists around, and *Guitar Player* magazine voted him Best New Guitarist of the Year in 1978.

Eddie's guitar innovations were used to powerful effect on Van Halen's next few LPs, as well as in the memorable high-speed solo he contributed to Michael Jackson's "Beat It" in 1982. Two years later, the band issued the highly acclaimed *1984* album, and despite the subsequent departure of lead vocalist David Lee Roth (he was replaced by Sammy Hagar), they went on to enjoy even greater commercial success in the late 1980s and early 1990s.

Van Halen's recent history has been more uncertain. Hagar left the group in 1996, and the band is presently without a permanent lead singer following the departure of his successor, Gary Cherone; there is current speculation that David Lee Roth may be invited to return. In April 2001, Eddie Van Halen confirmed that he had been receiving treatment for cancer. However, his playing has not been affected by his illness, and he has said there is a "good chance" that he will soon be free from the disease.

A typical Eddie Van Halen guitar solo may incorporate a bewildering range of sounds, including "dive bombs" and harmonics performed with a tremolo arm, "tapping" on the strings using both hands, and high-velocity riffing. In other words, a full-on sonic assault.

Stevie Ray Vaughan

1954–1990

Many blues guitar lovers still recall their shock and disbelief at the news of Stevie Ray Vaughan's death in a helicopter crash on August 27, 1990. He had been en route from a triumphant concert in Wisconsin (culminating in an onstage jam with Eric Clapton, Robert Cray, and Buddy Guy), and was at the zenith of his career after winning a Grammy for his *In Step* album, and completing a hugely successful U.S. tour. He had also recently been declared "Musician of the Decade" at a blues awards ceremony in Austin, Texas—the birthplace of his band, Double Trouble, at the end of the 1970s.

Stevie owed his fame to outstanding talent, years of hard work, and a few lucky breaks. Double Trouble was little known outside its home state until 1982, when renowned producer Jerry Wexler saw the band perform at a bar in Austin and arranged for them to appear at the prestigious annual jazz festival at Montreux, Switzerland. David Bowie caught their set and was so taken with the performance that he invited Stevie to guest on his album *Let's Dance* (1983). Legendary talent scout John Hammond Senior was similarly impressed by Double Trouble that night. Hammond, who had secured both Bob Dylan and Bruce Springsteen their first recording contracts, enthused about the band to Epic Records, who signed the band in 1984. Singer-songwriter Jackson Browne also saw the band's Montreux set and gave them free time to make an LP in his own studio. Double Trouble's debut *Texas Flood* and Bowie's *Let's Dance* both appeared the following year, vaulting Stevie Ray Vaughan to the attention of blues and rock fans worldwide.

Stevie's playing, as strongly influenced by Jimi Hendrix as by Albert King and other bluesmen, dominated the four remaining Double Trouble albums released during his lifetime. Like Hendrix, Stevie used a Fender Stratocaster and powerful amplification to produce a rich, overdriven tone. This gave a cutting edge to songs such as "Pride And Joy" (1983), on which he combined lead and rhythm in a single, up-front guitar part, and "The House Is Rockin'" (1989), with its raunchy, down-home feel. However, his sound and style were at their most characteristic during soaring, inventive solos such as that on "Texas Flood" (1983) and on the scintillating live version of the track released in 1986.

As well as his work with Double Trouble, Stevie's musical legacy includes the posthumously released *Family Style*, recorded in 1990 with his guitarist brother Jimmie, cofounder of another fine Texas blues band, The Fabulous Thunderbirds. Stevie's untimely death is all the more poignant given that he had recently emerged invigorated from a spell in a rehab clinic after years of endless touring and hard living. His newfound zest for life was reflected in the passion of the music he was making shortly before his death and there is little doubt that some of his best work was still to come.

Stevie Ray Vaughan's fiery take on the blues helped to reinvent the genre during the 1980s, earning him the respect and admiration of guitar greats such as Eric Clapton and B.B. King.

T-Bone Walker

Aaron Thibeaux ("T-Bone") Walker was born in Linden, Texas, on May 28, 1910. He grew up in Dallas with his parents, who were both blues fans and friends of touring players. As a child he met the legendary blues performer Blind Lemon Jefferson, and became the man's "eyes" whenever he was in town. Later, as a teenager, he became friends with Charlie Christian, with whom he shared his guitar teacher. T-Bone developed a style that incorporated rhythmic melodic runs and jazz-flavored chord changes and was one of the first blues-based musicians to "bend" strings to affect note phrasing. As a young man, he toured Texas during the late 1920s playing the blues, and won several talent competitions.

T-Bone moved to Los Angeles in 1934 and worked there during the late 1930s with "Big" Jim Wynn's band. Like Charlie Christian, he played an amplified guitar, which gave a distinctive feel to the band's overall sound. The band played regularly at local jazz venues, where T-Bone would often amaze crowds with tricks such as playing his guitar behind his head while doing the splits, in a spirit of showmanship that would later be revived by Chuck Berry, Jimi Hendrix, and Pete Townshend, among others. Walker recorded a series of hits for the Black & White label during the late 1940s including "T-Bone Shuffle," "I'm Gonna Find My Baby," and the famous "Stormy Monday." He refined his blues act while working with

Above: One sharp-dressed man. T-Bone onstage in his 1940s heyday.

experienced jazz musicians in the 1950s and 1960s, recording celebrated albums such as *Classics In Jazz* (1953), *T-Bone Walker* (1956), *T-Bone Blues* (1959), *Singing The Blues* (1960), *The Truth* (1968), *Funky Town* (1969), and *Feeling The Blues* (1969). His sophisticated "jazz-blues" style was a big influence on other musicians, including B.B. King, Freddie King, and Clarence "Gatemouth" Brown.

T-Bone carried on performing and recording well into the 1970s but he suffered a severe stroke in 1974 and died of bronchial pneumonia on March 16, 1975. Several compilation recordings have been released since his death.

Left: T-Bone Walker, showman par excellence. Such crowd-pleasing stunts belied Walker's masterful playing and sensitivity to the dynamic possibilities of the electric guitar.

Muddy Waters

McKinley Morganfield, born in the Mississippi Delta town of Rolling Fork, acquired the nickname "Muddy Waters" as a child, because he liked playing near a muddy creek. After his mother's death, he was brought up by his grandmother on a plantation near Clarksdale, and spent his early years working as a farm laborer while developing his musical skills. By his mid-twenties, he was an accomplished performer, strongly influenced by Delta blues artists such as Charley Patton and Son House.

In 1941 and 1942, folklorist Alan Lomax visited Muddy's home, and recorded his singing and playing for the Library of Congress. The experience of making these disks encouraged Muddy to leave the Delta and seek his fortune as a musician. In 1943, he moved to Chicago, and, after switching from acoustic to electric guitar, established himself on the city's club circuit, often sharing the stage with other ex-Delta bluesmen.

Above: In Chicago, Waters (shown here in 1970) developed a reinvigorated form of Delta slide guitar.

Waters's breakthrough came when he signed to Leonard Chess's Aristocrat label (later renamed after its founder). His first single for the company, "I Can't Be Satisfied," appeared in 1948, and was followed by a string of R&B hits that captured the authentic Delta feel of Waters's voice and guitar in an exciting new electric context. "Louisiana Blues" (1951), on which his eerie slide work is embellished by Little Walter Jacobs's harmonica, was among the most memorable of these, but it was the songs backed by a full band, including "I'm Your Hoochie Coochie Man" (1954), that proved to be the most influential. They established Waters as a leading figure on the Chicago scene, and inspired a new generation of blues and rock musicians—such as The Beatles, who, on their first visit to the United States, cited him as one of the Americans they most wanted to meet.

With the black audience for blues diminishing in the 1960s, Muddy developed a younger, predominantly white following. During the 1970s he played at U.S. and European music festivals, and continued to record regularly, developing a fruitful relationship with guitarist Johnny Winter, who produced Muddy's four final albums, released between 1977 and 1981. Muddy Waters died in his sleep in Chicago on April 30, 1983.

Left: Muddy Waters at the Newport Jazz Festival, 1960. Waters was pivotal in transforming acoustic Delta blues into the harder electric blues typical of urban centers.

John Williams

b.1941

John Williams, like his friend and fellow virtuoso Julian Bream, has broadened and enriched the repertoire of the classical guitar, and is acclaimed throughout the world as one of its foremost exponents. However, while Bream has devoted himself exclusively to Western art music, Williams has frequently (and sometimes controversially) involved himself in "crossover" projects. He has collaborated with performers from the fields of jazz and rock, achieving hit records in the process, while simultaneously maintaining a more conventional career on the concert platform.

Born in Melbourne, Australia, John Williams emigrated with his family to England in 1952. He was first taught guitar by his father Len, founder of the influential Spanish Guitar Centre in London. As a young man, John studied at the city's Royal College of Music; he also visited the Accademia Chigiana in Siena, for lessons with Andrés Segovia, returning there from 1957. Following his professional debut in 1958 at London's Wigmore Hall, he rapidly developed an international reputation as a soloist, widely respected for his economical style and for the clarity of his note playing. Williams excelled in his instrument's standard repertoire (including the Spanish pieces and Bach transcriptions popularized by Segovia), but during the 1960s he was to branch out increasingly into more unexpected musical territory.

Williams's interest in popular music was revealed on his LP *Changes* (1971), made with movie composer and arranger Stanley Myers, whose "Cavatina," used on the soundtrack of *The Deer Hunter* (1978), later gave the guitarist a hit single. In 1979, Williams became a member of Sky, a hybrid rock/classical group in which he played both acoustic Spanish and fingerstyle electric guitar. Despite sneers from purists, the band's records sold well, and he remained a member until 1984.

His involvement with Sky, and subsequently in jazz and folk, have never compromised John Williams's commitment to more formal music making. Since the 1970s, he has been active both in promoting new classical pieces and in championing unfamiliar and neglected ones, and has been closely associated with the work of two Latin-American guitarist-composers: Agustín Barrios (1885–1944), the Paraguayan "Paganini of the guitar," and Leo Brouwer (b.1939), from Cuba. He also played regularly in duos with Julian Bream until the late 1970s, and readily acknowledged the part that the older guitarist had played in popularizing the classical guitar.

Williams continues to maintain a busy schedule of tours, concerts, and recordings as a soloist as well as guest appearances with the Chilean group Inti-Illimani. He has also performed widely with his world music ensemble, John Williams and Friends.

John Williams has done much to broaden the appeal of the classical guitar, both through his solo work and via collaborations with rock, jazz, and world music performers.

Neil Young

b.1945

Born in Toronto, Canada, Neil Young began playing guitar during his teenage years, and was a member of the short-lived Mynah Birds (with future Motown star Ricky James) before moving to California in early 1966. After his arrival in Los Angeles, Young met an old friend, guitarist Steve Stills, whom he joined in the critically lauded band Buffalo Springfield. The group's three albums gave Neil's songwriting skills and distinctive guitar style—sometimes gentle, but often fierce and fuzz-laden—an early chance to shine.

Following the band's breakup, Young issued his first two solo LPs in 1969. The second of these, *Everybody Knows This Is Nowhere*, marked the start of his lengthy collaboration with backing band Crazy Horse. However, during this period Young was also appearing with other musicians—he worked with Crosby, Stills, and Nash in concert and on record—and releasing two predominantly acoustic solo albums, *After The Goldrush* (1970) and *Harvest* (1972), both of which featured folk-style picking and country inflections. The albums were substantial hits, making Young one of the most successful singer-songwriters to emerge in the early 1970s.

Young's next records did not match the massive commercial success of their predecessors, and a dark, depressive atmosphere pervades much of his output in the years after Crazy Horse guitarist Danny Whitten's death from a drug overdose in 1972. However, *Zuma* (1975), made with a new Crazy Horse lineup featuring guitarist Frank Sampedro, heralded a new direction, and the group subsequently accompanied Young on his 1978 "Rust Never Sleeps" North American tour. These shows, captured on *Live Rust* (1979), combined solo acoustic performances with searing, visceral treatments of songs such as "Cortez The Killer" and "When You Dance I Can Really Love." The impressively distorted guitar work on such tracks, characterized by Young's seething, fractured lead lines, would later earn him the title "godfather of grunge."

Young released a stylistically diverse (and often bewilderingly inconsistent) series of albums during the 1980s, including poorly received experiments with synthesizers and vocoders. However, he regained the approval of both critics and fans with *Freedom* (1989), which included his anthemic "Rockin' In The Free World," and *Ragged Glory* (1990). The latter, recorded with Crazy Horse, featured a set of urgent, powerful songs, and the return of Young's trademark blistering guitar solos.

In recent years, Young has alternated between acoustic projects, such as the pastoral *Harvest Moon* (1992), and rockier outings, including *Mirror Ball* (1995) with Seattle grunge pioneers Pearl Jam. Young remains an influential, splendidly unpredictable force on the current music scene.

Although Neil Young has played folk-style acoustic guitar on much of his work, it is his startling, unpredictable electric solos on which his reputation as a guitarist rests.

Frank Zappa

1940–1993

The young Frank Zappa's diverse musical tastes were not those of most mid-1950s American teenagers. His fascination with avant-garde classical composers such as Edgard Varèse (1883–1965) sat strangely with his passion for the raucous R&B soloing of Johnny "Guitar" Watson and Guitar Slim, and the sounds of doo-wop vocal harmony. However, these ingredients all helped to shape Zappa's unique playing and composing style, and to equip him for his self-appointed artistic mission "to plug… the gaps between so-called serious music and so-called popular music."

Zappa grew up in Southern California, and Los Angeles was the base from which, in 1964, he launched The Mothers (the suffix "of Invention" was added later, at the insistence of an innuendo-sensitive record label). Their first album, *Freak Out!* (1966), was a sneering, surreal attack on hippie sensibilities, social conditioning, and other targets to which Zappa would often return on subsequent projects. The scathing lyrical barbs were set to strange, inspired music ranging from ingenious parodies of 1950s and 1960s pop to montages of electronically modified sound.

The record was a remarkable debut, but Zappa's playing skills and subtle use of effects were more clearly showcased on later albums, such as *Hot Rats* (1969), which includes his classic, wah-wah-inflected solo on "Willie The Pimp." With his preference for the harsh, edgy tones used by his R&B heroes, Zappa could be a bitingly intense soloist, but sometimes took a mellower approach, as on "Blessed Relief" from *The Grand Wazoo* (1972). Seeing himself more as a composer than a guitarist, he made extensive use of spontaneity and improvisation when performing live, rarely executing his instrumentals in exactly the same way twice. He was assiduous in recording these onstage solos, some of which he later compiled and released on *Shut Up 'N' Play Yer Guitar* (1981), a 3-CD set that provides a comprehensive overview of Zappa's unique style as a guitarist. The hard rock tour de force "Five-Five-Five" and the blindingly fast "Heavy Duty Judy" are just two of the many highlights contained on the album.

Also active as a composer of orchestral, chamber, and electronic music, Zappa often complained that he seldom had time for guitar practice. However, his technique never appeared to suffer from his extended periods away from the instrument, and his reputation as one of the most innovative players in the history of rock seems secure.

Frank Zappa's extraordinary capacity for work continued unabated throughout his career, even after the announcement in 1991 that he had prostate cancer. He died from the disease in Los Angeles on December 4, 1993, leaving behind a body of work characterized by both its stunning variety and its offbeat, inimitable humor.

Head Mother. Frank Zappa's off-kilter sense of humor belied a serious interest in melding avant-garde, classical, jazz, and rock music, as well as a prodigious guitar-playing talent.

Index

Figures in **bold** indicate main entries.